HAL LEONARD PIANO REPERTOIRE
Elementary Through Intermediate

JOURNEY THROUGH THE
CLASSICS
COMPLETE

COMPILED AND EDITED BY JENNIFER LINN

CONTENTS

Cover Art: Rose Garden, 1876 (oil on canvas) by Claude Monet (1840-1926)
Private Collection/ Photo © Lefevre Fine Art Ltd., London/ The Bridgeman Art Library
Nationality / copyright status: French / out of copyright
Adaptation by Jen McClellan

ISBN 978-1-4768-7433-3

7777 W. BLUEMOUND RD. P.O. BOX 13819 MILWAUKEE, WI 53213

In Australia Contact:
Hal Leonard Australia Pty. Ltd.
4 Lentara Court
Cheltenham, Victoria, 3192 Australia
Email: ausadmin@halleonard.com.au

Visit Hal Leonard Online at
www.halleonard.com

BOOK 1
Elementary

CONTENTS

BOOK 2
Late Elementary

CONTENTS

BOOK 3
Early Intermediate

CONTENTS

BOOK 4
Intermediate

CONTENTS

JOURNEY THROUGH THE
CLASSICS

BOOK 1
Elementary

BOOK 1 • ELEMENTARY
Reference Chart

WHEN COMPLETED	PAGE	TITLE	COMPOSER	ERA	KEY	METER	CHALLENGE ELEMENTS
	8	RENAISSANCE DANCE	Praetorius	Baroque	C	4/4	Eighth notes & slurs
	9	FOLLOW THE LEADER	Köhler	Romantic	C	4/4	Eighth notes in imitation
	9	LITTLE MARCH	Türk	Classical	C	4/4	RH in treble C; eighth notes and slurs
	10	ALLEGRO	Reinagle	Classical	C	2/4	RH in treble C; 2-note slurs; D.C. al Fine
	11	VIVACE	Gurlitt	Romantic	C	4/4	RH in treble C; LH harmonic intervals
	12	THE BRAVE HORSEMAN	Vogel	Romantic	C	4/4	RH shift in treble; RH/LH coordination, syncopation
	13	HUNTING HORNS	Gurlitt	Romantic	C	4/4	Staccato; harmonic interval slurs
	14	CLASSIC MINUET	Linn	Classical	F	3/4	F major key signature; 6ths; 3/4 time signature
	15	ROMANCE	Wohlfahrt	Romantic	Dm	3/4	D minor key signature; dynamic control
	16	SHEPHERD'S FLUTE	Salutrinskaya	Romantic	Dm	4/4	D minor key signature; RH in 𝄢; damper pedal
	17	MINUET IN C	Hook	Classical	C	3/4	RH/LH coordination; triplet rhythm
	18	LYRICAL ETUDE	Beyer	Romantic	G	4/4	G major key signature; LH accompaniment & balance
	19	ETUDE IN G	Czerny	Classical	G	4/4	G major key signature; LH alberti bass
	20	THE PENNYWHISTLE	Türk	Romantic	G	4/4	C♯ accidental; RH/LH coordination
	20	PROCESSION	Reinagle	Classical	G	4/4	Staccato/legato coordination; hand shifts
	22	MINUET	Reinagle	Classical	C	3/4	RH hand shifts; staccato/legato coordination
	23	LITTLE BIRD	Gurlitt	Romantic	C	2/4	Both hands in 𝄞; staccato/legato coordination
	24	MELODY	Diabelli	Classical	C	4/4	Both hands in 𝄞; ties in LH voicing
	25	DANCE	Gurlitt	Romantic	C	3/4	Both hands in 𝄞; balance in melody/accompaniment
	26	ETUDE IN E MINOR	Gurlitt	Romantic	Em	4/4	E minor key signature; LH alberti bass
	28	LITTLE WALTZ	Gurlitt	Romantic	F	3/4	Balance in melody/accompaniment; hand shifts
	30	GAVOTTA	Hook	Classical	C	4/4	Staccato/legato coordination; dynamic echo
	32	BAGATELLE	Diabelli	Classical	G	3/4	LH harmonic intervals and 3-note chords
	33	BOURRÉE IN D MINOR	Graupner	Baroque	Dm	¢	D minor key signature, articulation & coordination
	34	MENUET EN RONDEAU	Rameau	Baroque	C	3/4	RH scale passages & contrapuntal skills

Renaissance Dance

Michael Praetorius
(1571–1621)

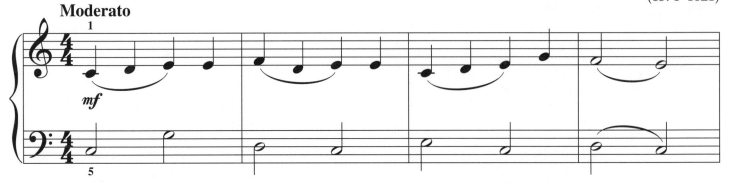

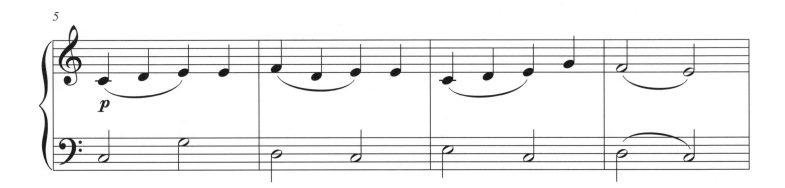

Follow the Leader

Louis Köhler
(1820–1886)

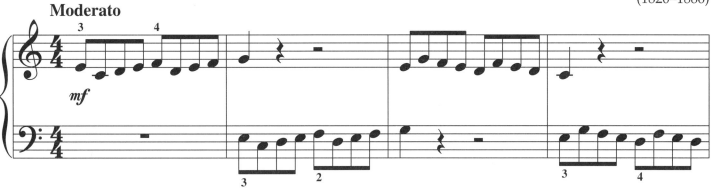

Little March

Daniel Gottlob Türk
(1750–1813)

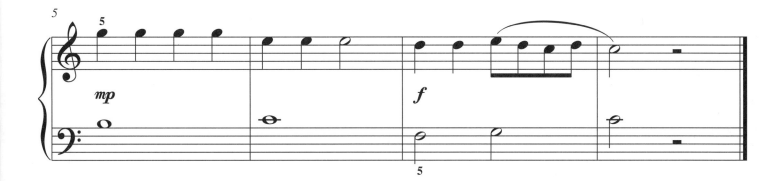

Allegro

Alexander Reinagle
(1756–1809)

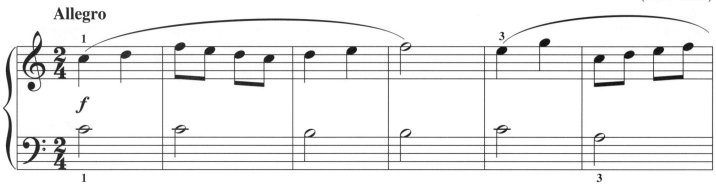

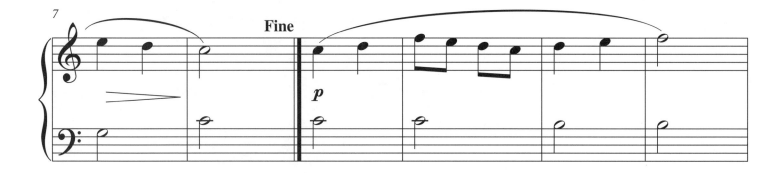

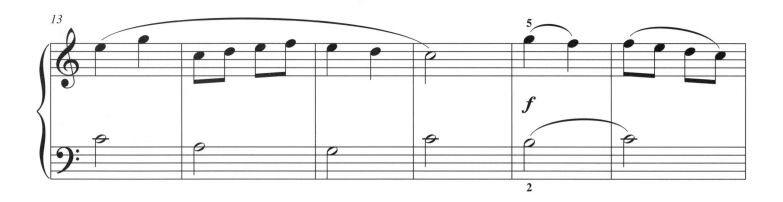

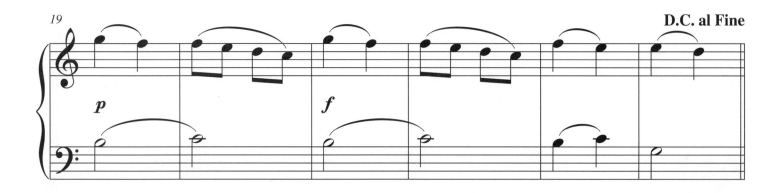

Vivace
Op. 117, No. 8

Cornelius Gurlitt
(1820–1901)

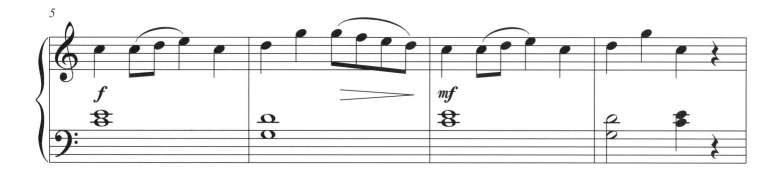

The Brave Horseman

Moritz Vogel
(1846–1922)

Marcia con forza

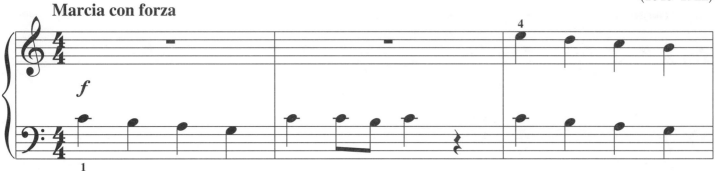

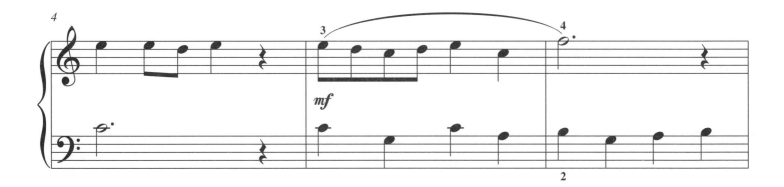

Hunting Horns

Op. 117, No. 10

Corneluis Gurlitt
(1820–1901)

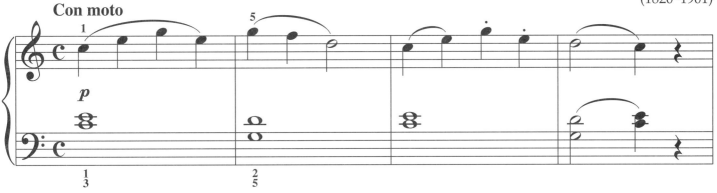

Classic Minuet

Jennifer Linn
(1960–)

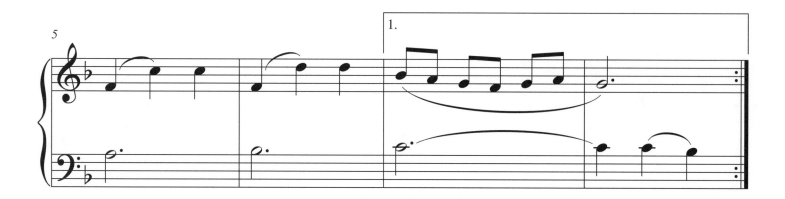

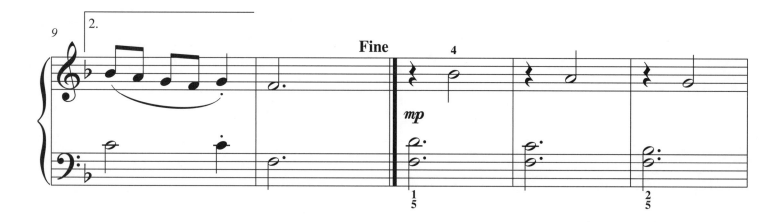

Romance

Heinrich Wohlfahrt
(1797–1883)

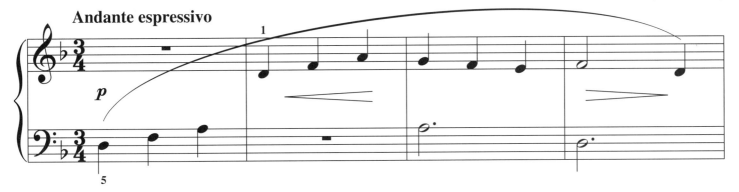

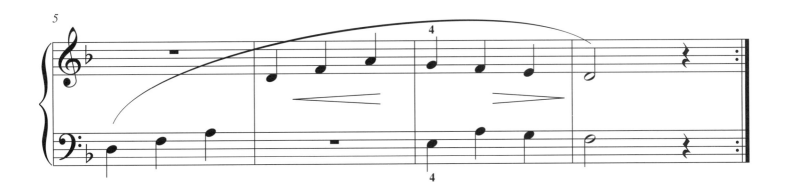

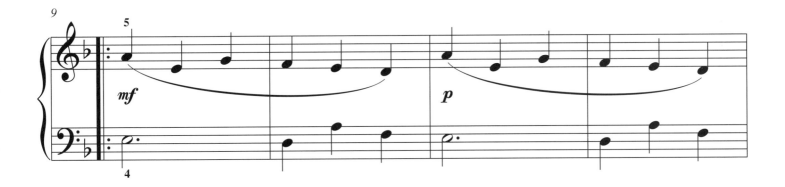

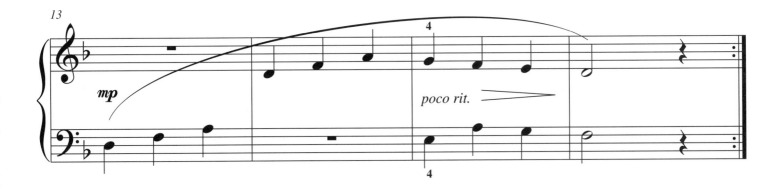

Shepherd's Flute

Tat'iana Salutrinskaya
(unknown)

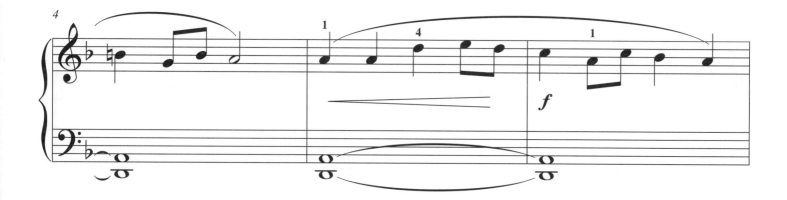

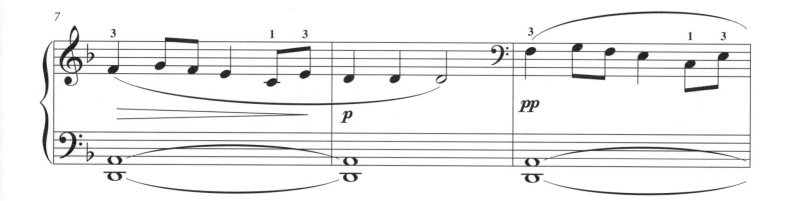

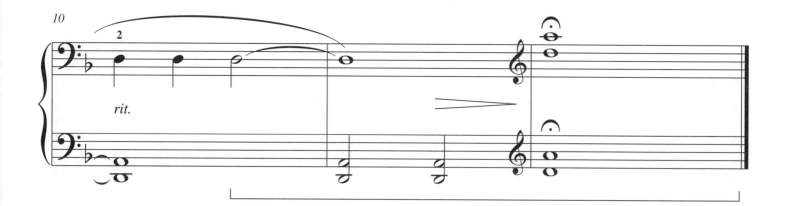

Minuet in C

James Hook
(1746–1827)

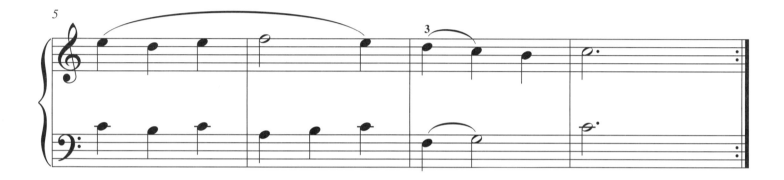

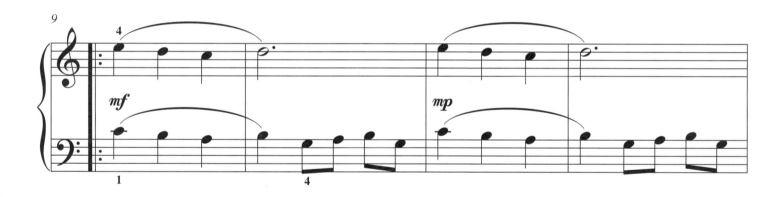

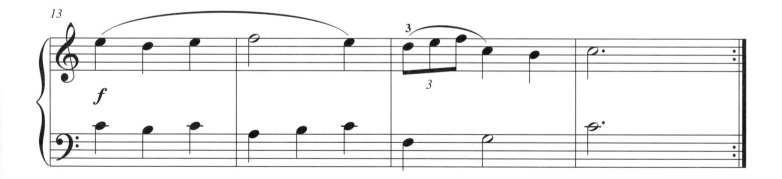

Lyrical Etude
Op. 101, No. 39

Ferdinand Beyer
(1803–1863)

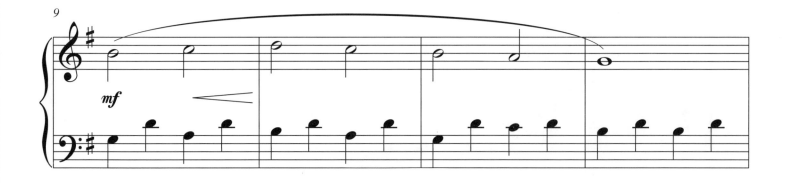

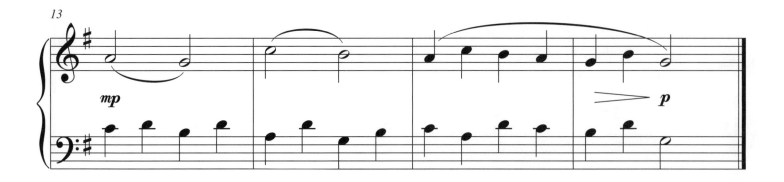

Etude in G
Op. 823, No. 11

Carl Czerny
(1791–1857)

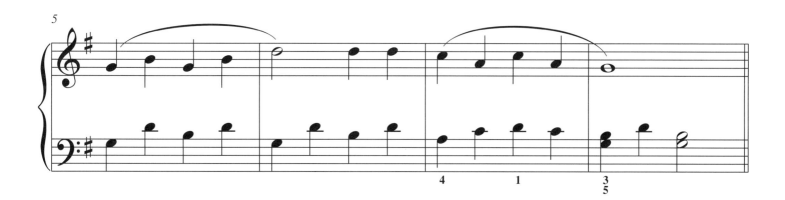

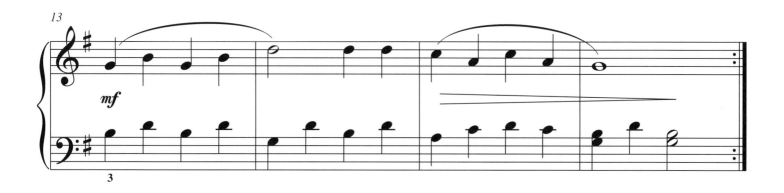

The Pennywhistle

Daniel Gottlob Türk
(1756–1813)

Allegro moderato

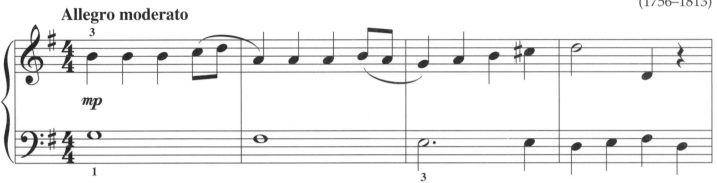

Procession

Alexander Reinagle
(1756–1809)

Andante

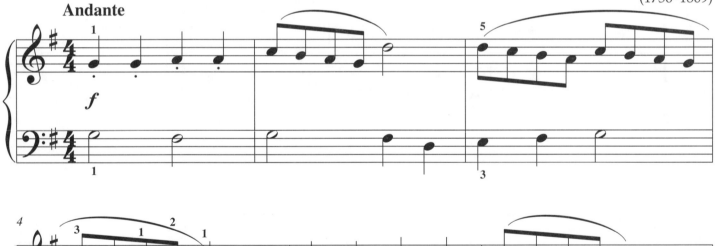

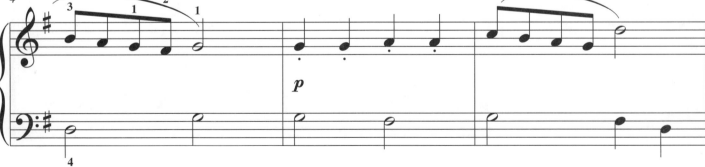

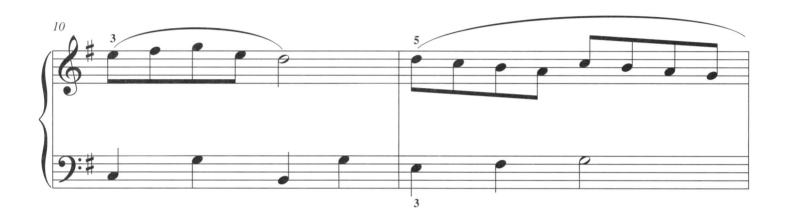

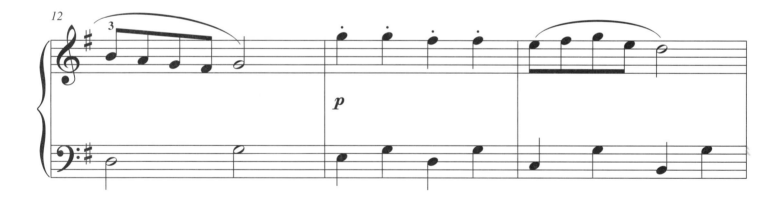

Minuet

Alexander Reinagle
(1756–1809)

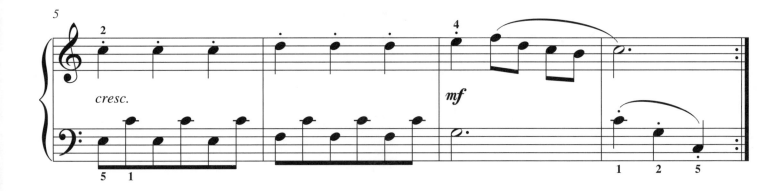

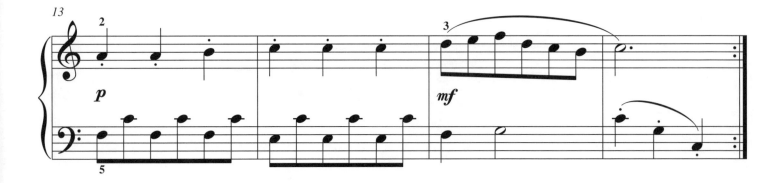

Little Bird
Op. 117, No. 7

Cornelius Gurlitt
(1820–1901)

Melody

Anton Diabelli
(1781–1858)

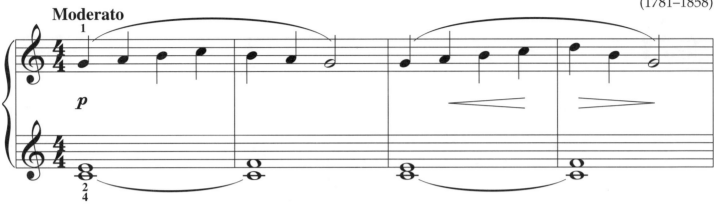

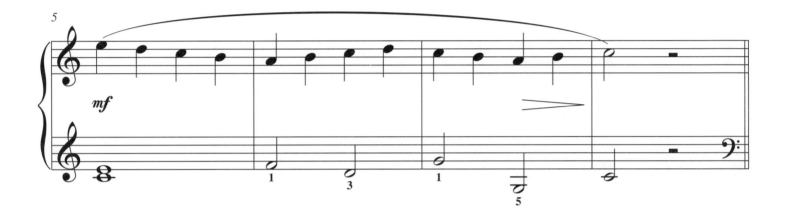

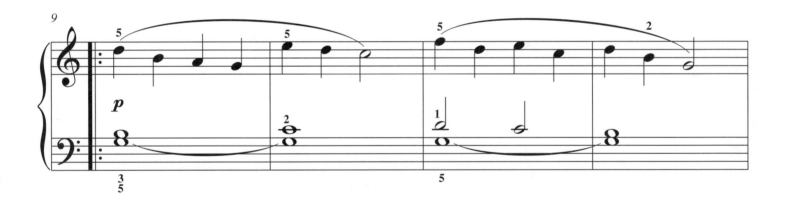

Dance

Cornelius Gurlitt
(1820–1901)

Etude in E Minor
Op. 82, No. 35

Cornelius Gurlitt
(1820-1901)

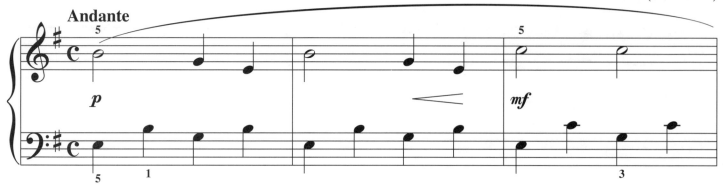

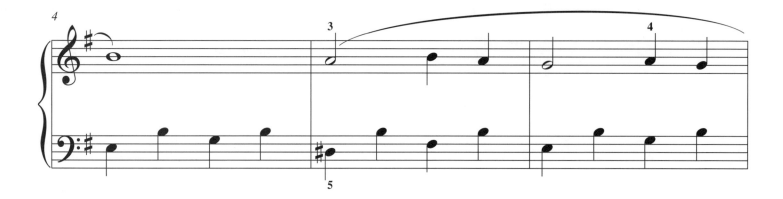

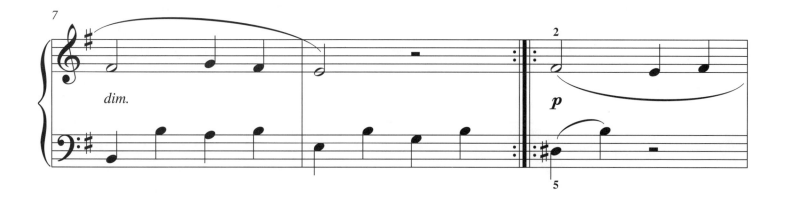

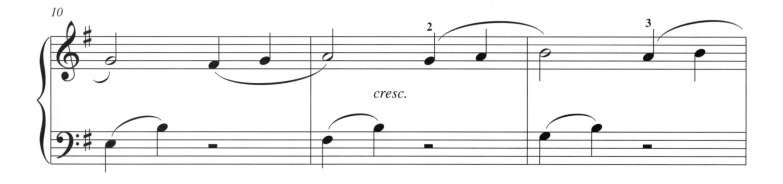

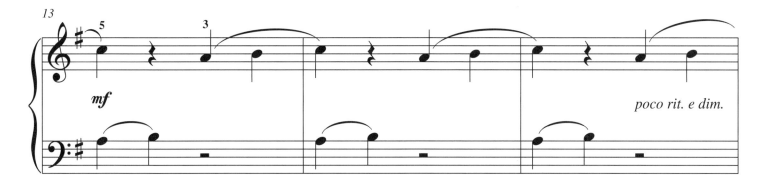

poco rit. e dim.

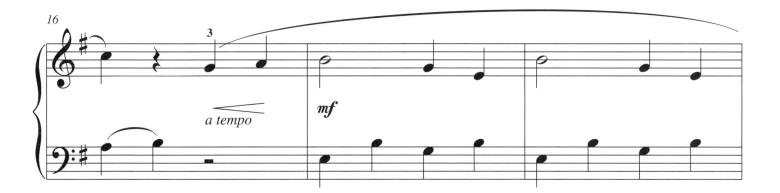

a tempo

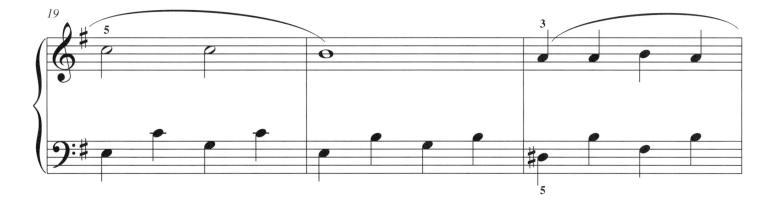

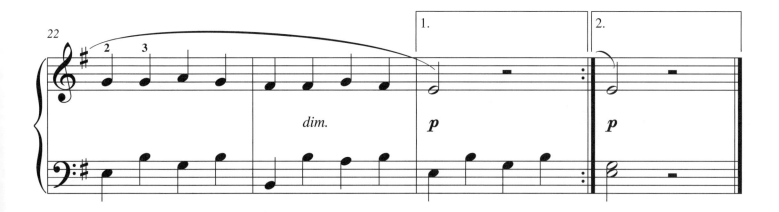

Little Waltz

Cornelius Gurlitt
(1820–1901)

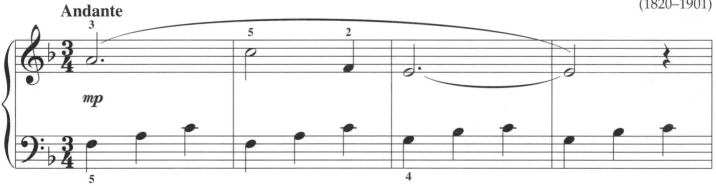

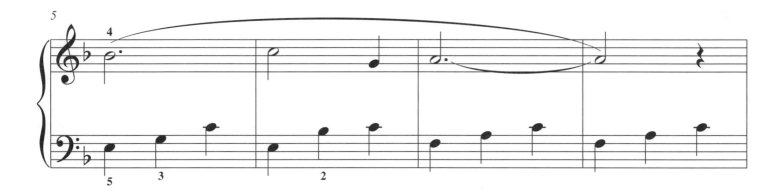

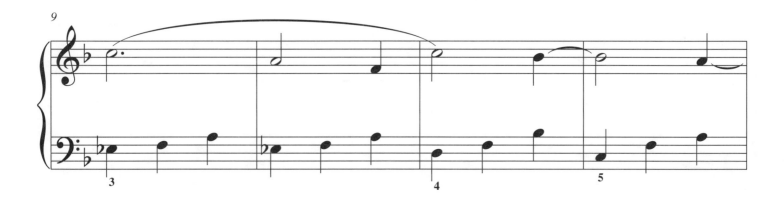

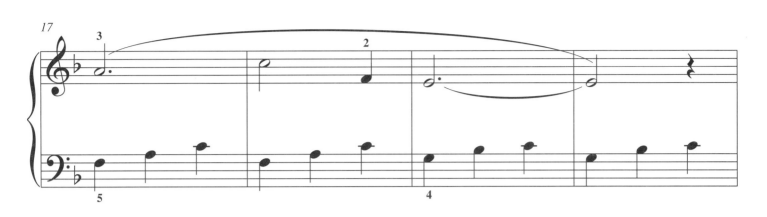

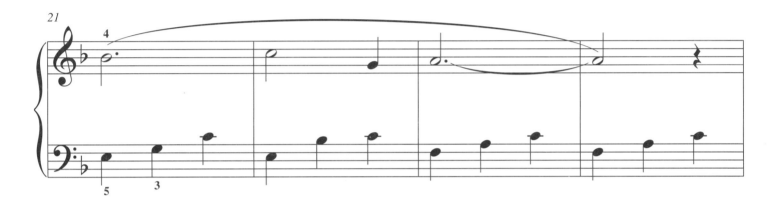

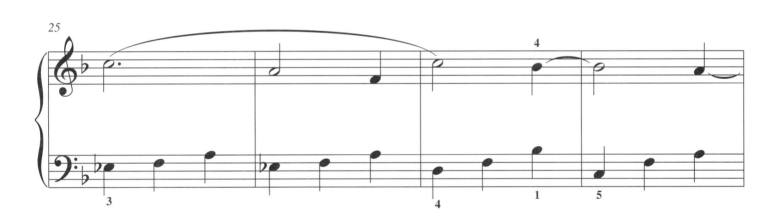

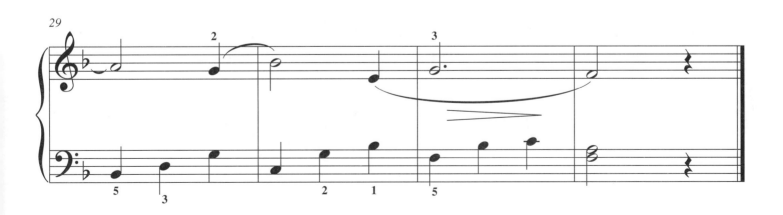

Gavotta
Op. 81, No. 3

James Hook
(1746–1827)

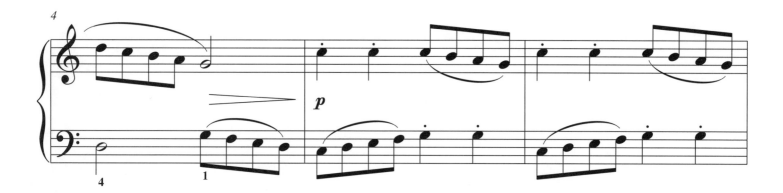

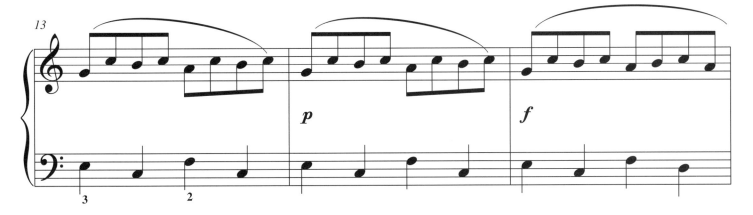

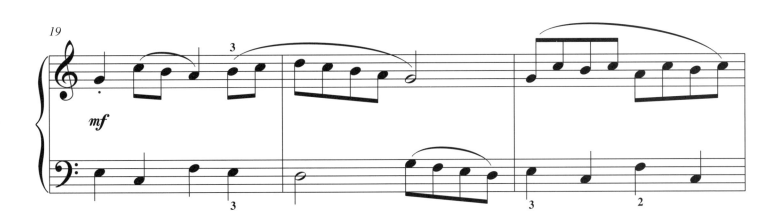

Bagatelle

Anton Diabelli
(1781–1858)

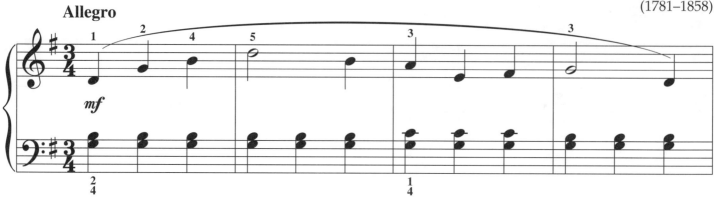

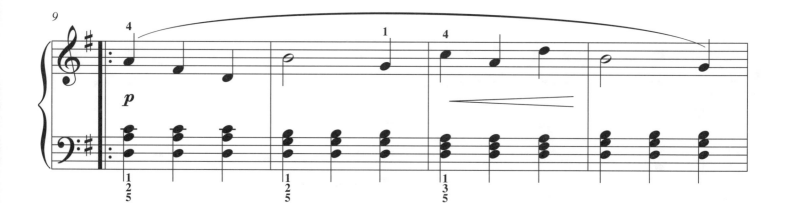

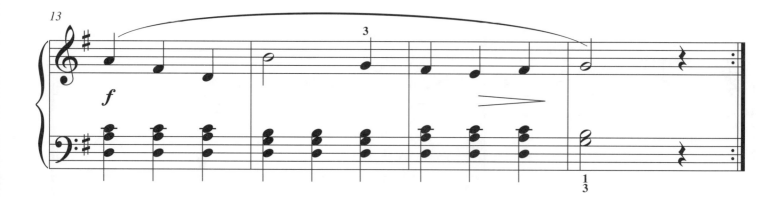

Bourrée in D Minor

Christoph Graupner
(1683–1760)

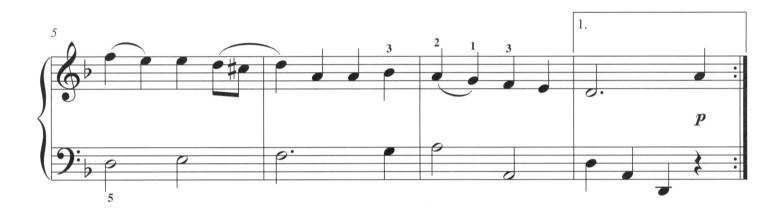

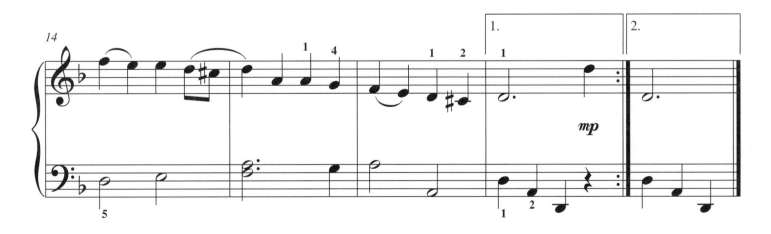

Menuet en Rondeau

Jean-Phillipe Rameau
(1683–1764)

Allegretto

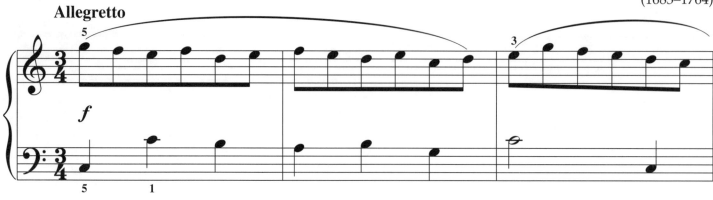

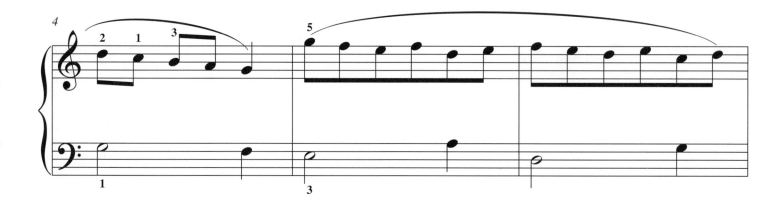

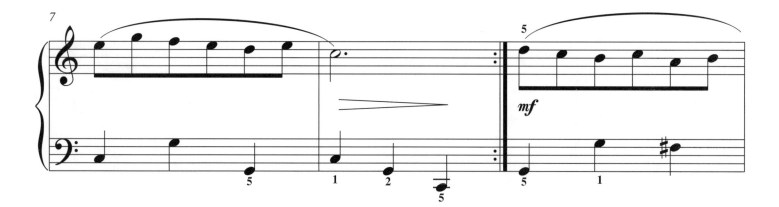

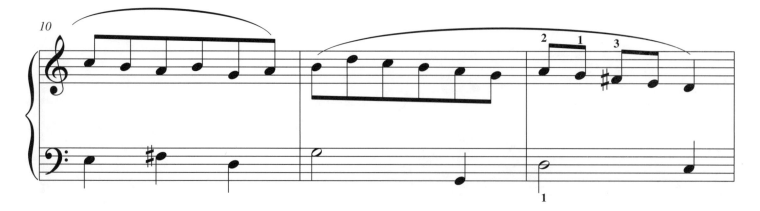

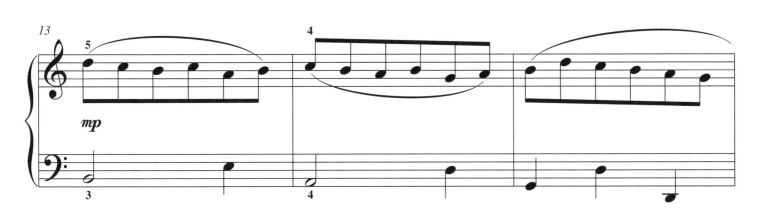

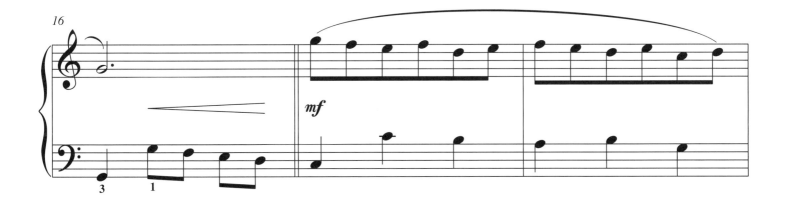

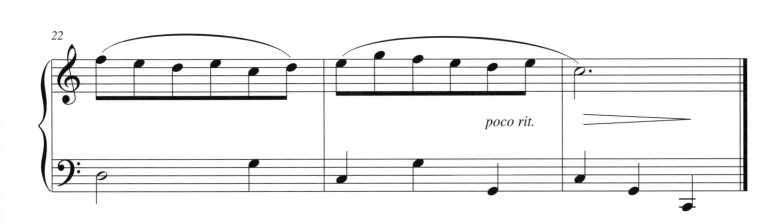

JOURNEY THROUGH THE
CLASSICS

BOOK 2
Late Elementary

BOOK 2 · LATE ELEMENTARY
Reference Chart

WHEN COMPLETED	PAGE	TITLE	COMPOSER	ERA	KEY	METER	CHALLENGE ELEMENTS
	38	Russian Folk Song	Beethoven	Classical	G	$\frac{2}{4}$	Dotted rhythm; legato/staccato coordination
	39	Sonatina in C	Duncombe	Baroque	C	$\frac{2}{4}$	Triplet and duplet rhythms; RH finger substitution
	40	Minuet in G	Telemann	Baroque	G	$\frac{3}{4}$	Triplet and duplet rhythms; portato touch
	41	Menuet in F	Mozart, L.	Classical	F	$\frac{3}{4}$	Hand shifts; LH octaves; echo dynamics
	42	Trumpet Tune	Duncombe	Baroque	C	$\frac{3}{4}$	Repeated notes and harmonic thirds; hand position extension
	44	Waltz	Vogel	Romantic	G	$\frac{3}{4}$	Balance between melody & accompaniment; connecting pedal
	46	Little Sonata	Wilton	Classical	C	$\frac{4}{4}$ & $\frac{3}{4}$	Accents; syncopation; echo dynamics; RH/LH coordination
	48	Melody (Arabian Air)	Le Couppey	Romantic	Am	$\frac{2}{4}$	Legato touch; phrasing; 16th notes; fermata
	50	Minuet in G	Bach, J.S.	Baroque	G	$\frac{3}{4}$	Articulation; contrapuntal skills; crossing 3 over 1
	52	Morning Prayer	Gurlitt	Romantic	C	¢	Vertical reading; Connecting pedal; both hands in 𝄢
	54	Bagatelle	Diabelli	Classical	C	$\frac{3}{8}$	3/8 time signature; balance between melody & accompaniment
	55	Tarantella	Lynes	Romantic	Am	$\frac{6}{8}$	6/8 time signature; fast legato scales in RH/staccato in LH
	56	Giga	Arnold	Classical	C	$\frac{6}{8}$	Fast and continuous scale patterns in RH
	58	Musette	Le Couppey	Romantic	G	¢	Drone bass; articulation; RH scale patterns with finger crossings
	60	Scotch Dance	Kuhlau	Classical	C	$\frac{2}{4}$	Alberti bass; sforzando chords; coordination between hands
	61	Burleske	Mozart, L.	Classical	G	$\frac{2}{4}$	Broken LH octaves; 16th notes; articulation
	62	Menuet in G	Petzold	Baroque	G	$\frac{3}{4}$	Articulation; finger crossing and contrapuntal skills
	64	Menuet in F	Mozart, W.A.	Classical	F	$\frac{3}{4}$	Finger substitution; articulation; triplet rhythm
	66	Church Bells	Camidge	Classical	C	$\frac{2}{4}$	Vertical reading; connecting pedal; both hands in 𝄢
	67	Bright Sky	Gurlitt	Romantic	C	$\frac{2}{4}$	Alberti bass with shifts; both hands in 𝄢; repeated notes
	70	Sad at Heart	Fuchs	Romantic	Am	$\frac{3}{4}$	Phrasing and balance; pedal; voicing; expression
	71	Sarabande	Pachelbel	Baroque	B♭	$\frac{4}{4}$	B-flat Key signature; vertical reading; connecting pedal
	72	Distant Bells	Streabbog	Romantic	C	$\frac{4}{4}$	Crossing LH over RH; connecting pedal; accents; balance
	74	Night Escape	Gurlitt	Romantic	Dm	$\frac{4}{4}$	LH melody with RH repeating harmonic seconds and thirds

Russian Folk Song

Ludwig van Beethoven
(1770–1827)

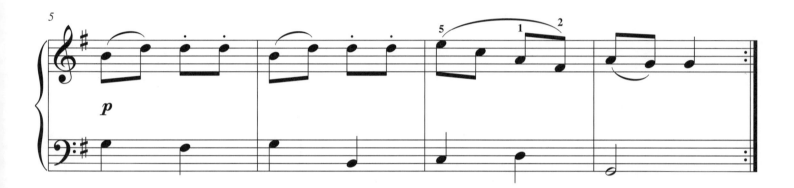

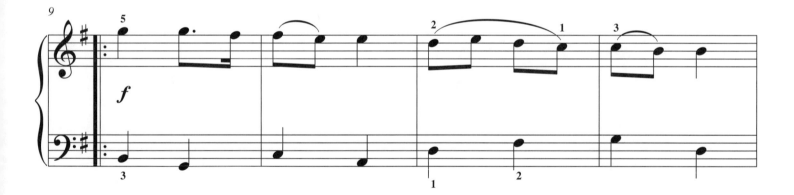

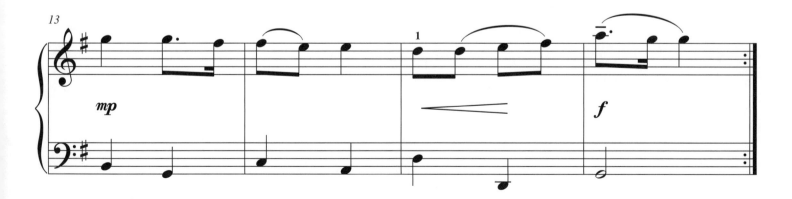

Sonatina in C Major

William Duncombe
(1690–1769)

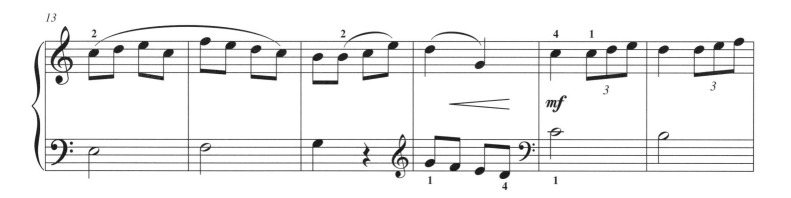

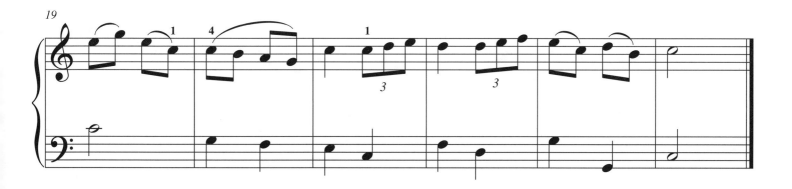

Minuet in G Major

Georg Philipp Telemann
(1681–1767)

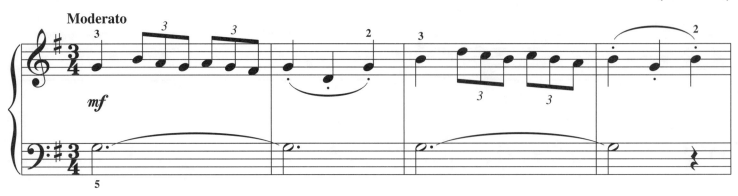

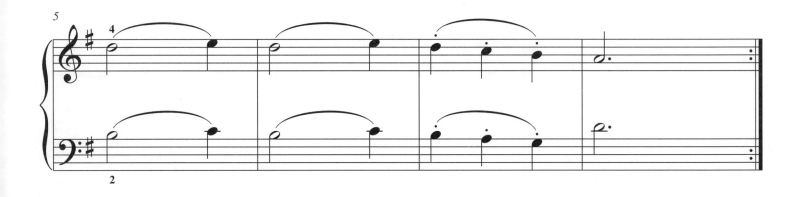

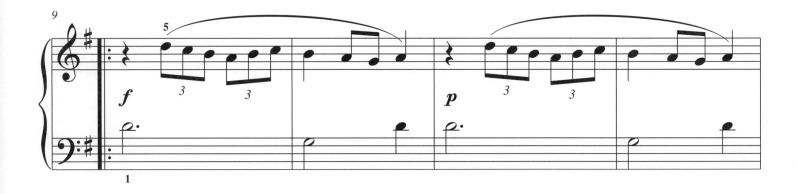

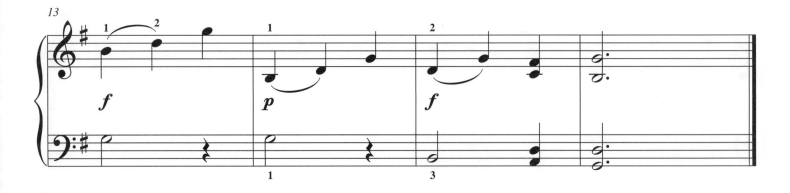

Menuet in F Major

Leopold Mozart
(1719–1787)

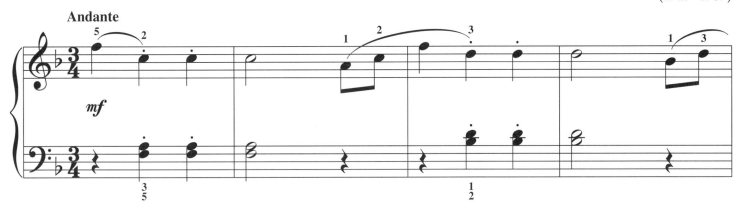

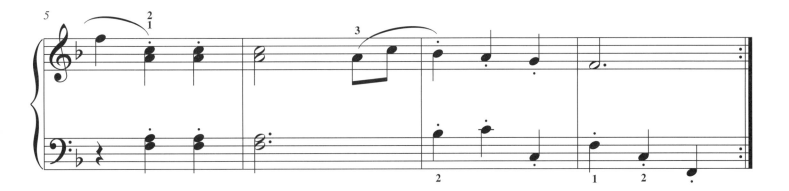

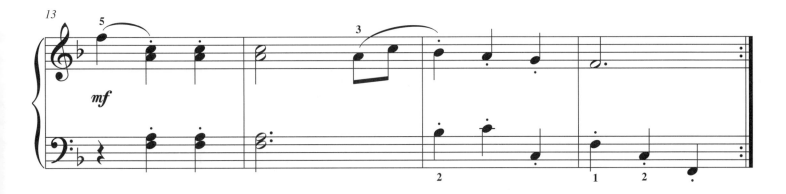

Trumpet Tune

William Duncombe
(1690-1769)

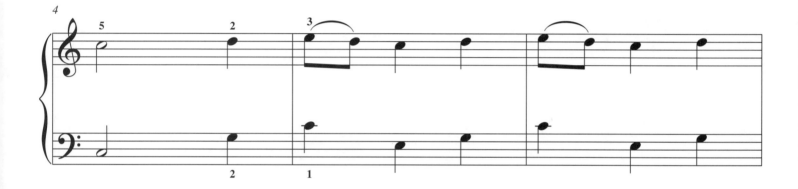

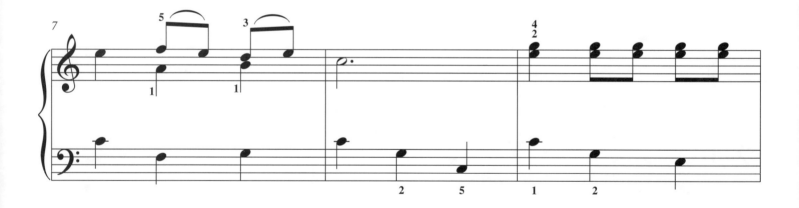

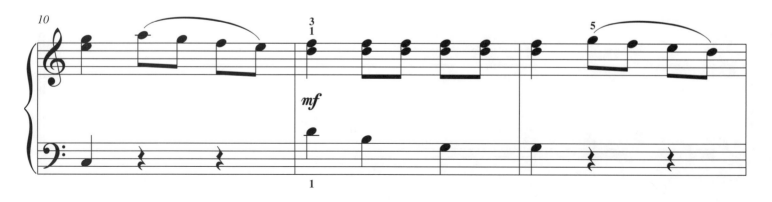

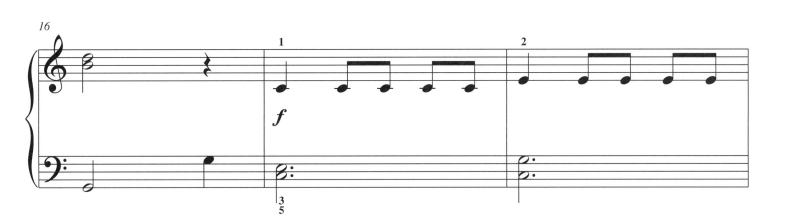

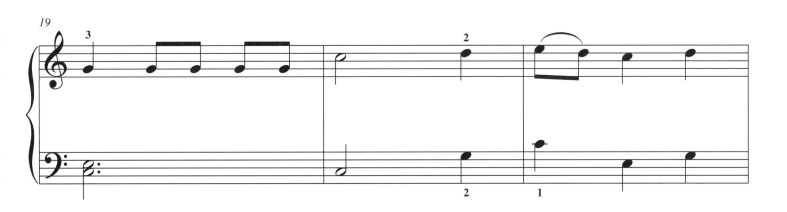

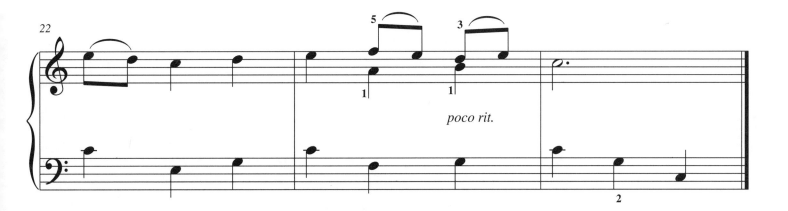

Waltz

Moritz Vogel
(1846–1922)

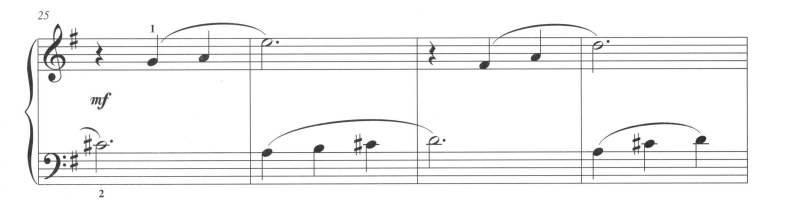

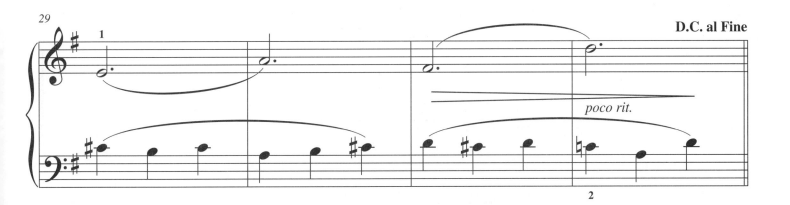

Little Sonata

I.

Charles H. Wilton
(1761–1832)

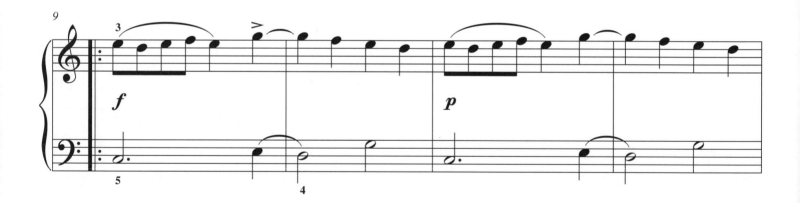

II.

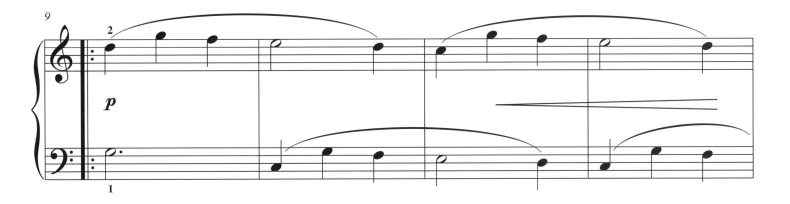

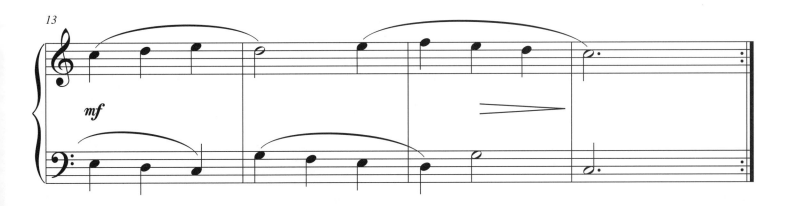

Melody
(Arabian Air)

Félix Le Couppey
(1811–1887)

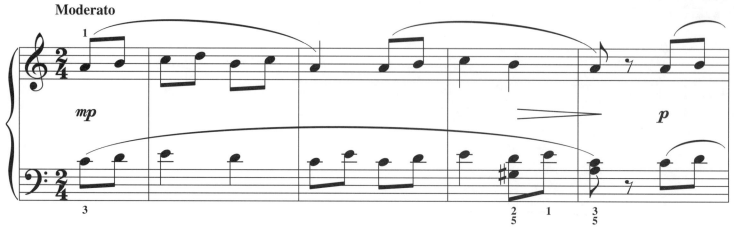

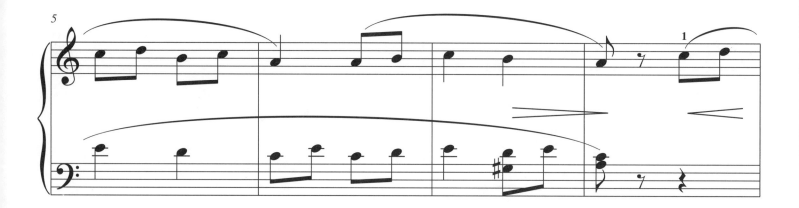

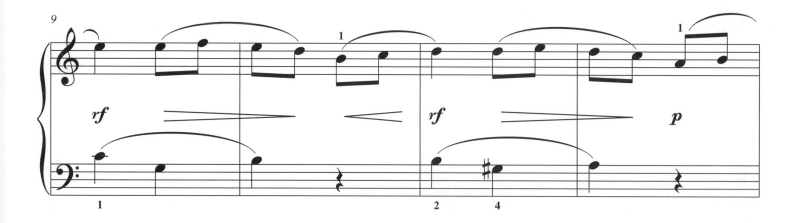

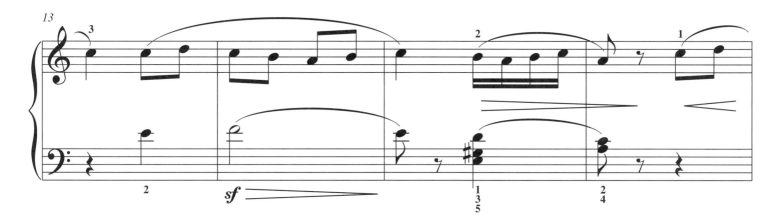

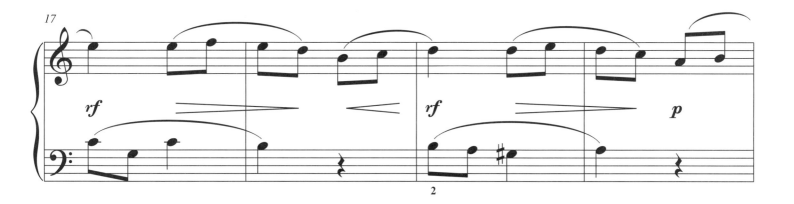

Minuet in G Major
BWV 822

Johann Sebastian Bach
(1685–1750)

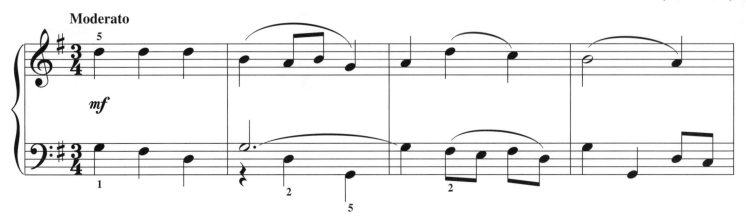

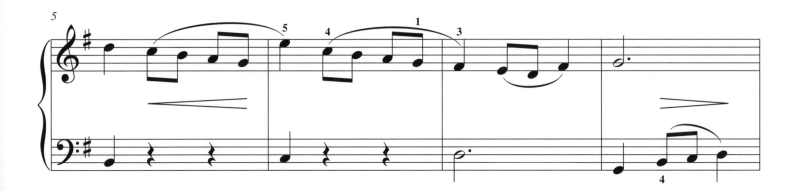

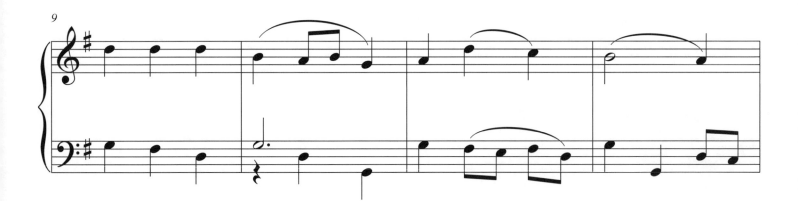

Morning Prayer

Op. 101, No. 2

Cornelius Gurlitt
(1820–1901)

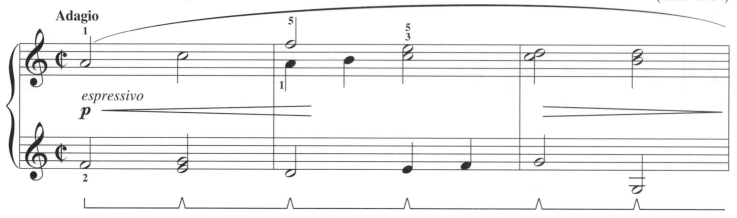

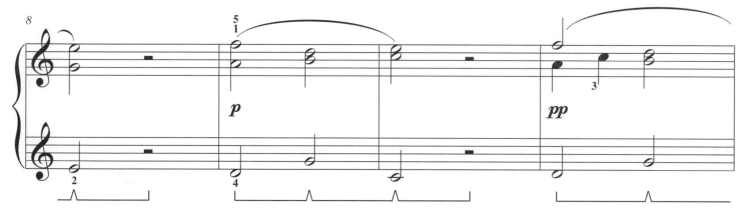

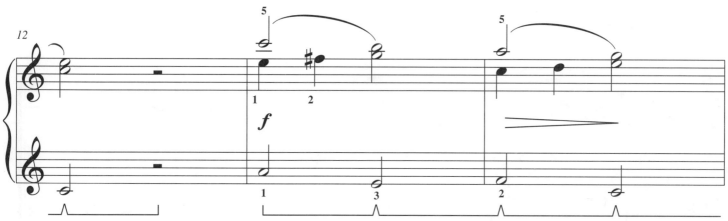

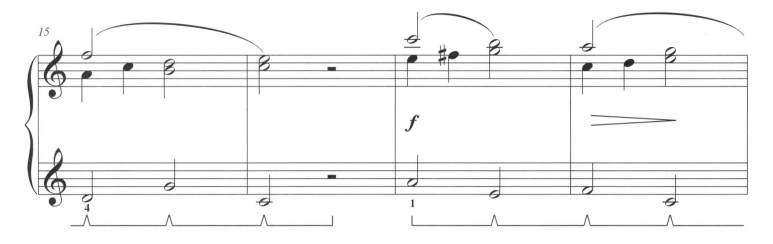

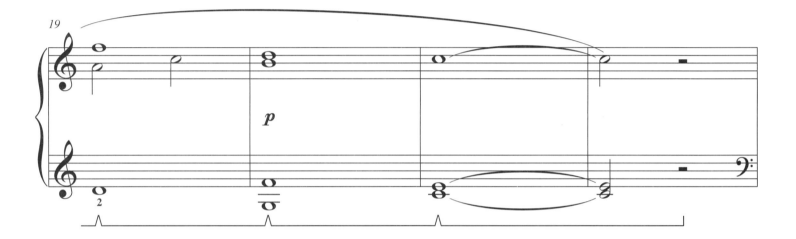

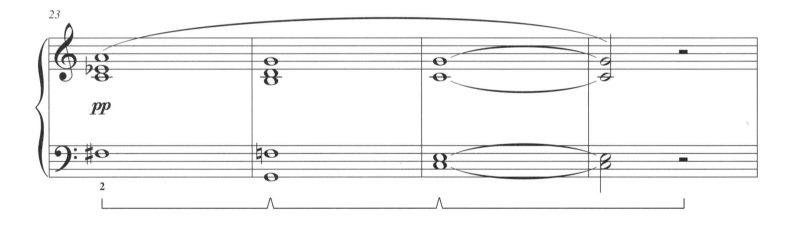

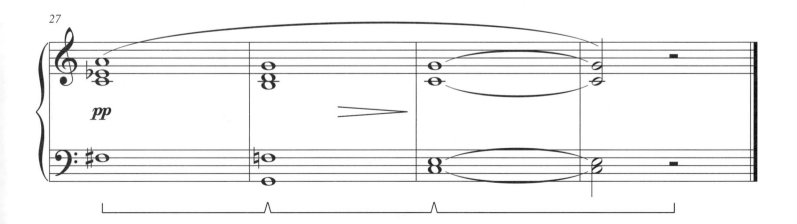

Bagatelle

Anton Diabelli
(1781–1858)

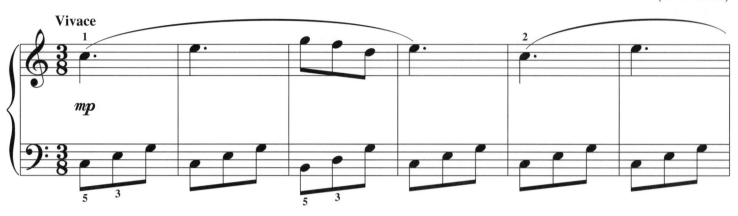

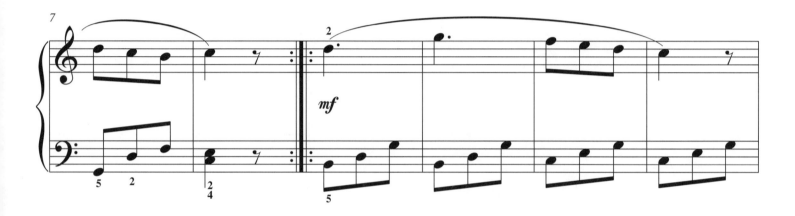

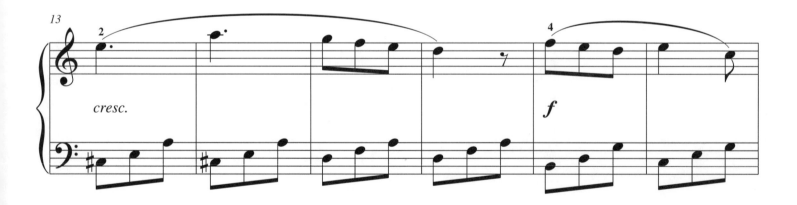

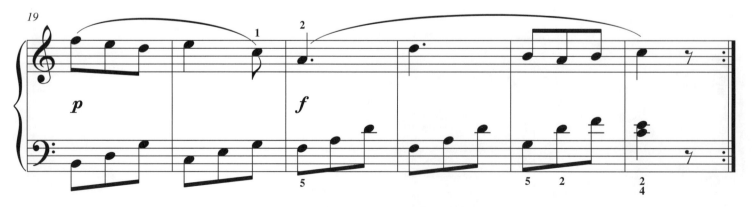

Tarantella
Op. 14, No. 8

Frank Lynes
(1858–1913)

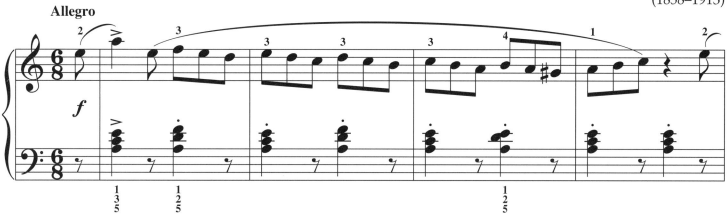

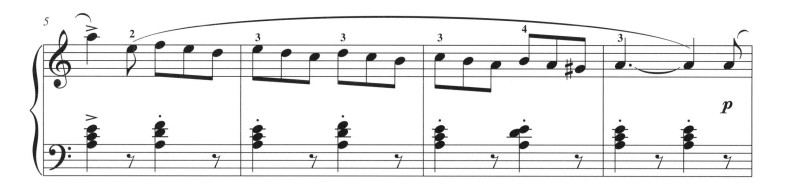

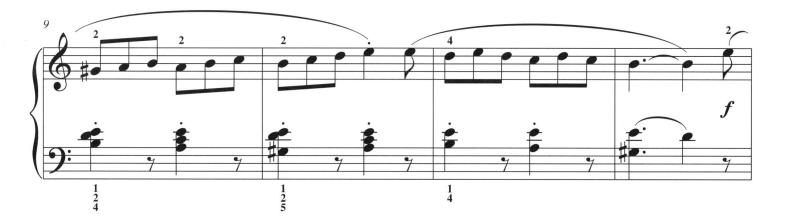

Giga

Samuel Arnold
(1740–1802)

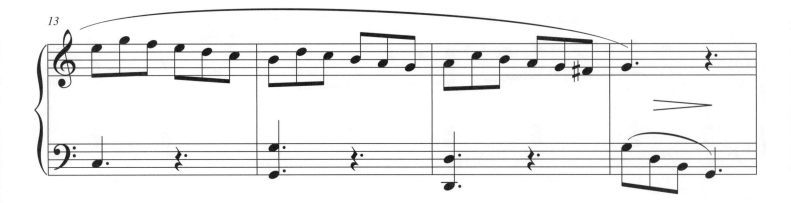

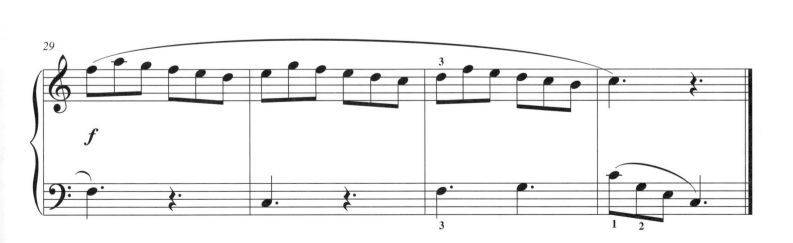

Musette

Félix Le Couppey
(1811-1887)

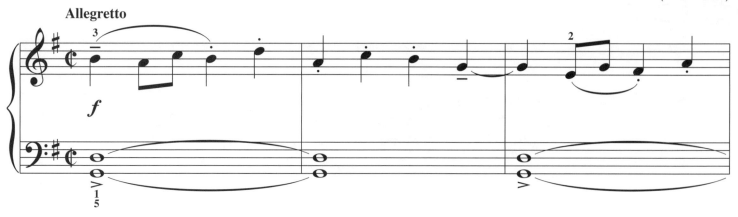

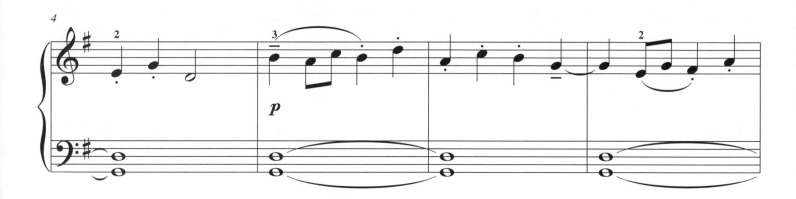

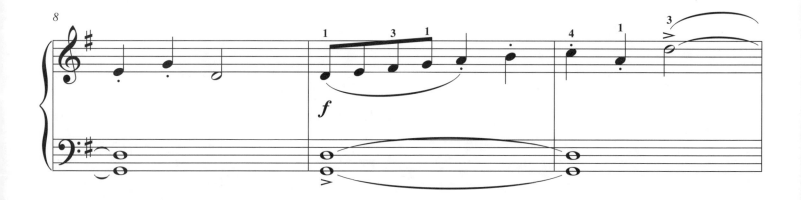

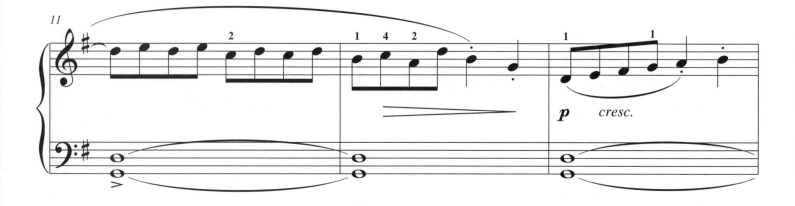

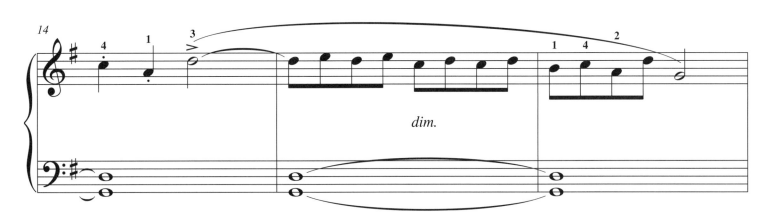

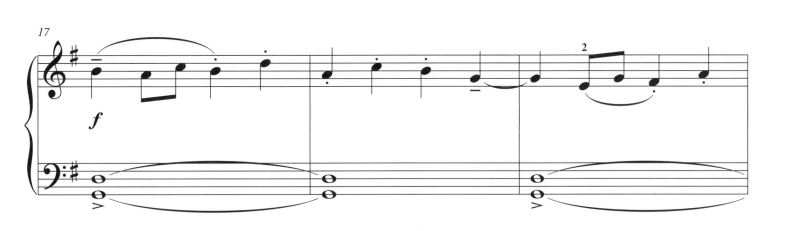

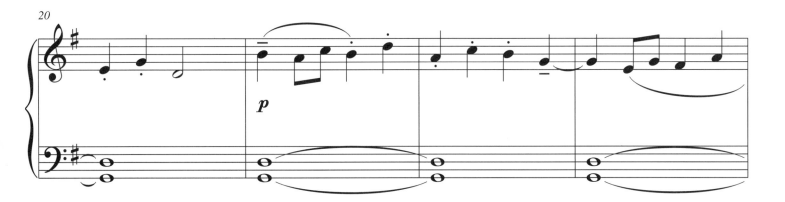

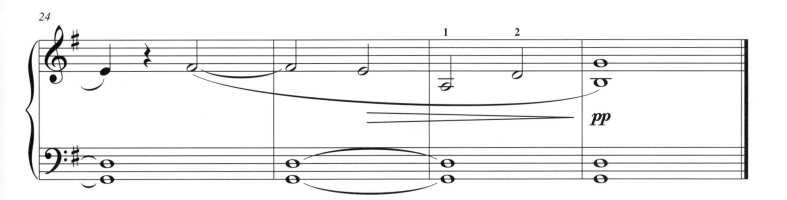

Scotch Dance

Friedrich Kuhlau
(1787–1832)

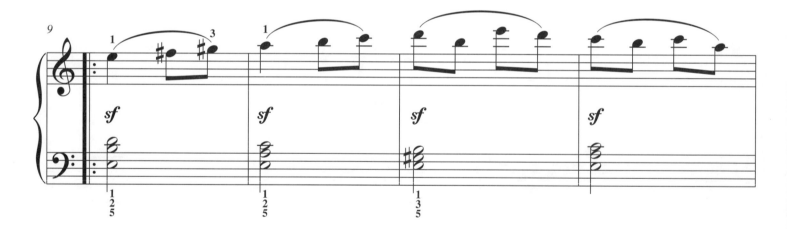

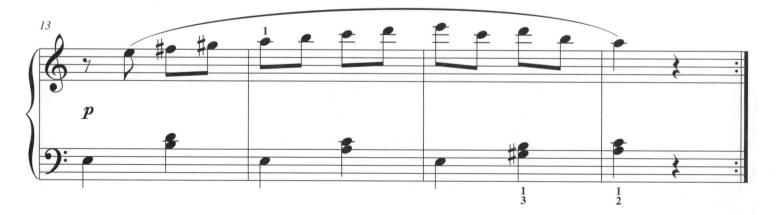

Burleske

Leopold Mozart
(1719-1787)

Menuet in G Major

Christian Petzold
(1677–1733)

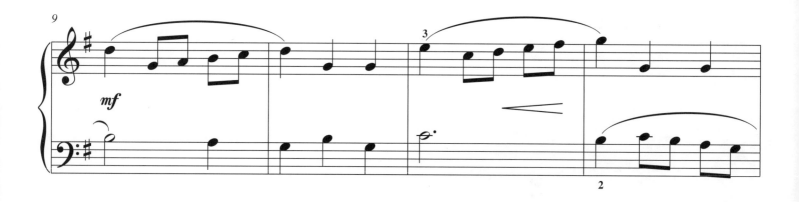

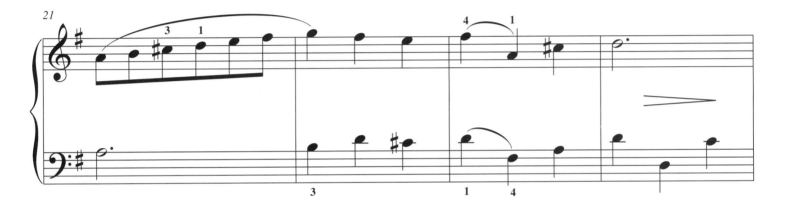

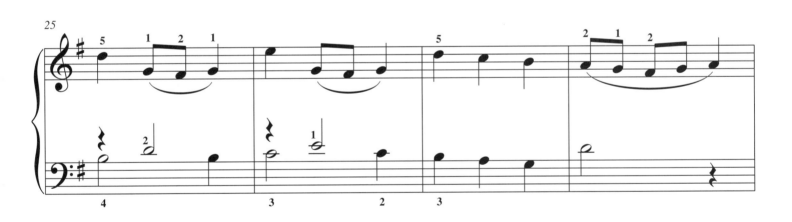

Menuet in F Major

Wolfgang Amadeus Mozart
(1756–1791)

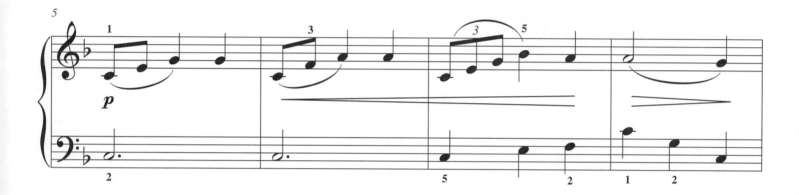

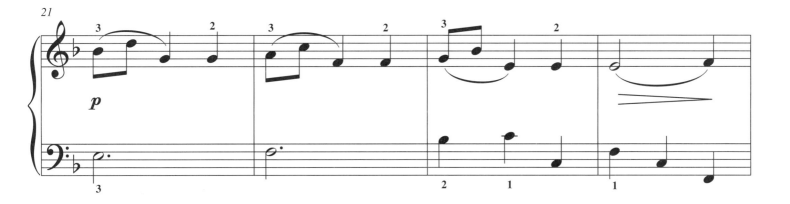

Church Bells

Matthew Camidge
(1758–1844)

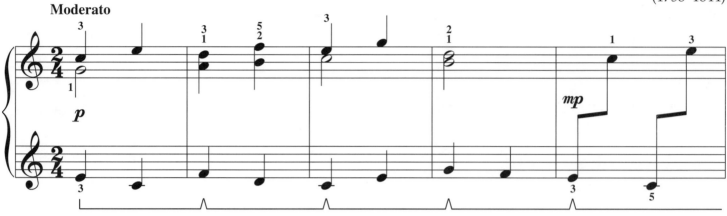

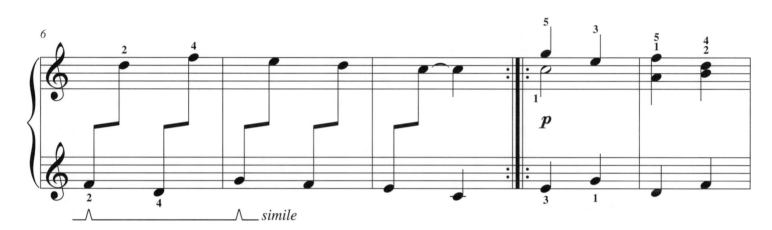

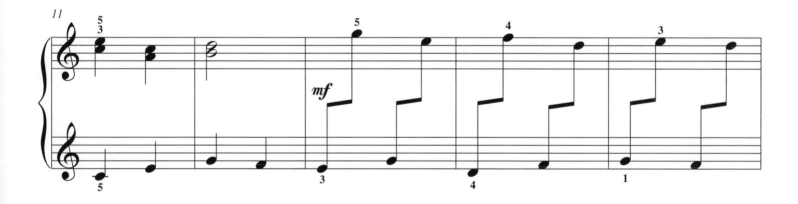

Bright Sky
Op. 140, No. 3

Cornelius Gurlitt
(1820-1901)

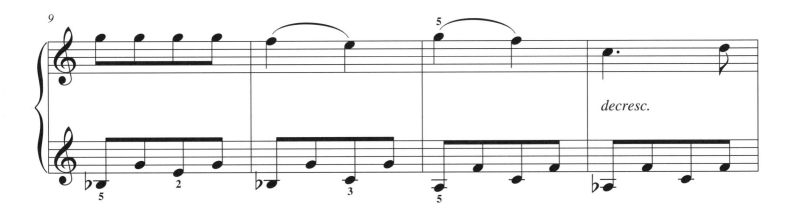

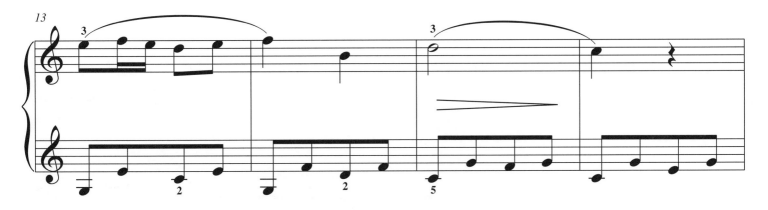

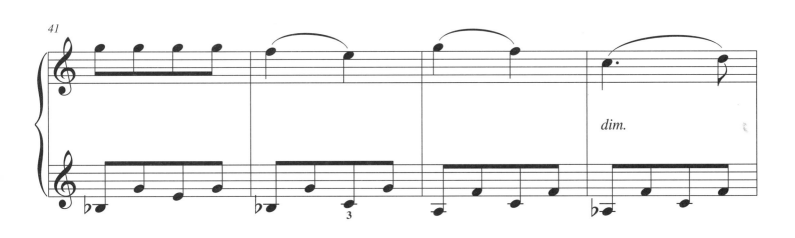

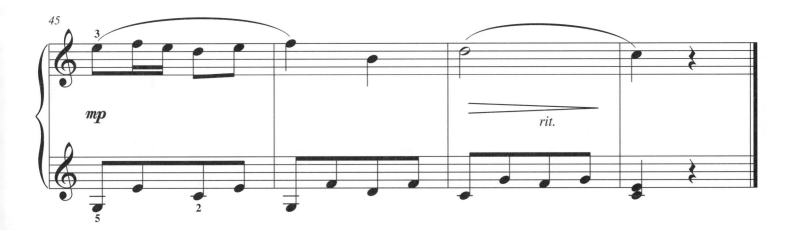

Sad at Heart

Op. 47, No. 5

Robert Fuchs
(1847–1927)

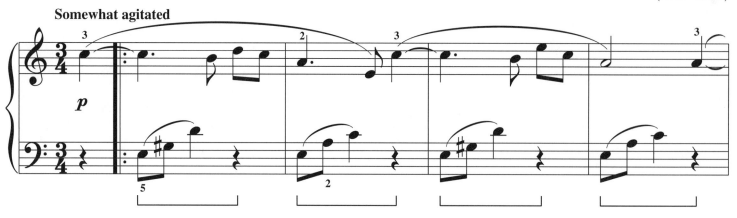

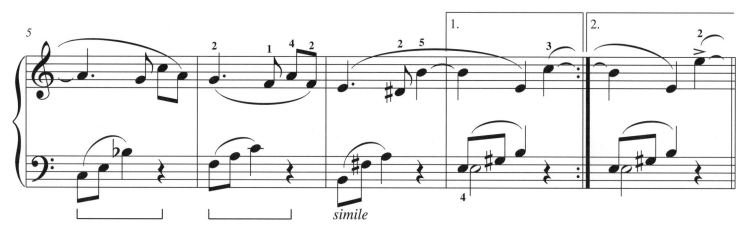

Sarabande

Johann Pachelbel
(1653–1706)

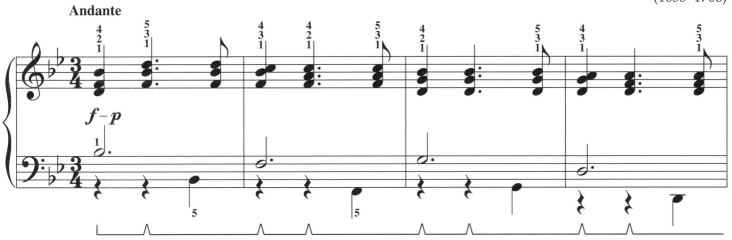

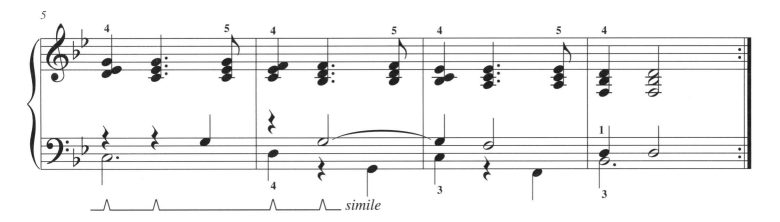

Distant Bells
Op. 63, No. 6

Louis Streabbog
(1835-1886)

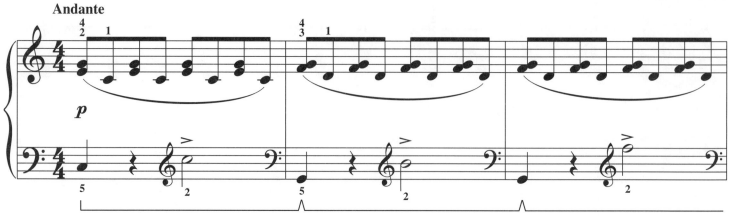

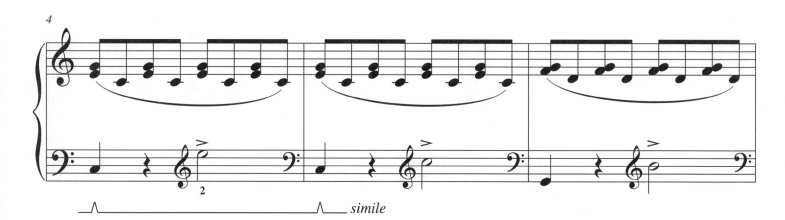

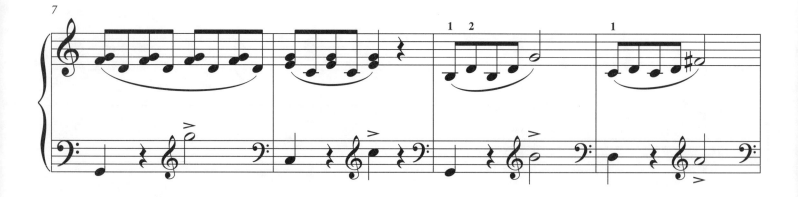

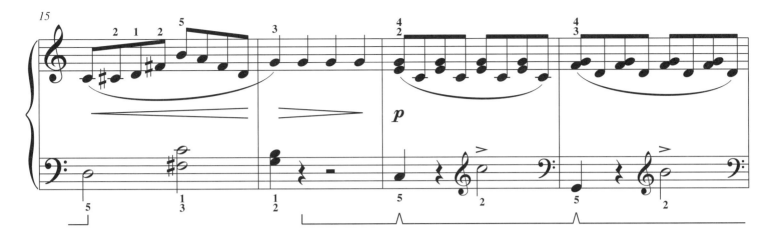

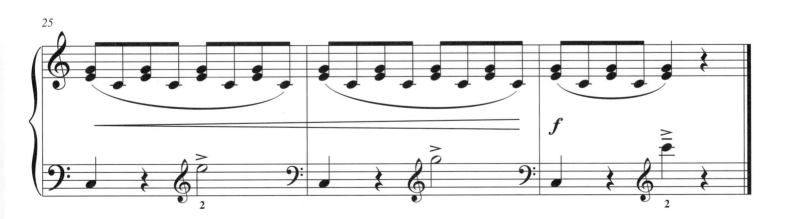

Night Escape
Op. 82, No. 65

Cornelius Gurlitt
(1820-1901)

Allegro non troppo

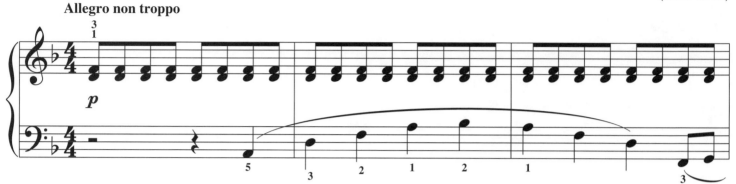

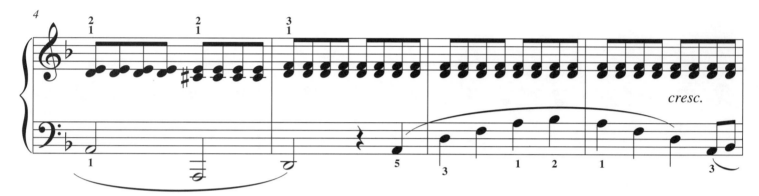

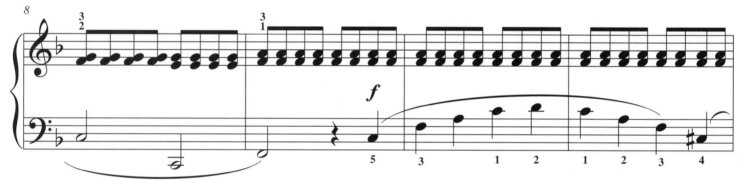

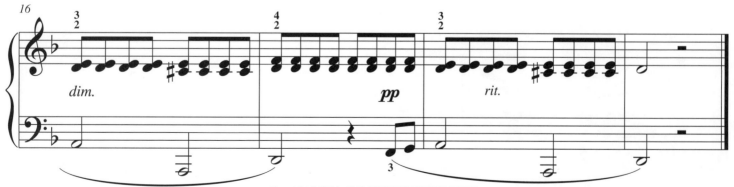

JOURNEY THROUGH THE
CLASSICS

BOOK 3
Early Intermediate

BOOK 3 · EARLY INTERMEDIATE
Reference Chart

✔ WHEN COMPLETED	PAGE	TITLE	COMPOSER	ERA	KEY	METER	CHALLENGE ELEMENTS
	77	Etude	Czerny	Classical	C	$\frac{4}{4}$	Both hands in 𝄞; repeated notes in LH; legato harmonic intervals
	78	Arabesque	Burgmüller	Romantic	Am	$\frac{2}{4}$	16th notes; RH and LH shifts; legato/staccato coordination
	80	Humming Song	Schumann	Romantic	C	$\frac{3}{4}$	Both hands in 𝄞; legato touch; balance and melody/accompaniment in one hand
	82	Russian Folk Song	Beethoven	Classical	Am	$\frac{2}{4}$	Vertical reading; shifting chords
	83	The Bear	Rebikoff	Romantic	C	$\frac{2}{4}$	Both hands in 𝄢; broken LH octaves; reading accidentals
	84	Musette	Bach (notebook)	Baroque	D	$\frac{2}{4}$	D major key signature; 16th notes; quick hand shifts; legato/staccato coordination
	86	Sonatina in G	Attwood	Classical	G	$\frac{4}{4}$	Alberti bass; legato/staccato coordination; articulation and phrasing
	88	Ecossaise	Beethoven	Classical	G	$\frac{2}{4}$	Broken LH octave shifts; 16th notes; syncopation; D.C. al Fine
	89	Tarantella	Spindler	Romantic	C	$\frac{3}{8}$	$\frac{3}{8}$ time signature; very fast scale passages; legato/staccato coordination
	92	Russian Polka	Glinka	Romantic	Dm	$\frac{2}{4}$	16th notes; frequent LH shifts; accents; legato/staccato coordination
	93	Spanish Dance	Oesten	Romantic	Am	$\frac{3}{4}$	16th notes; repeating LH chords; accents; articulation
	94	Sonatina in C	Latour	Classical	C	$\frac{4}{4}$	Continuous scale patterns; LH/RH coordination
	96	Wild Rider	Schumann	Romantic	Am	$\frac{6}{8}$	Fingerings in broken chord patterns; staccato touch; frequent hand shifts
	98	Theme and Variation	Gurlitt	Romantic	G	$\frac{2}{4}$	Connecting pedal; portato touch; phrasing; triplets; balance
	100	Sonatina in C	Clementi	Classical	C	¢	Scale passages; alberti bass; broken arpeggios in both hands; articulation
	102	Minuet and Trio	Mozart, W.A.	Classical	G	$\frac{3}{4}$	Articulation and phrasing; triplets; 16th notes; frequent hand shifts
	104	Menuet in D Minor	Bach (notebook)	Baroque	Dm	$\frac{3}{4}$	Contrapuntal style; frequent hand shifts; leaping intervals; LH/RH coordination
	106	Solfeggio	Bach, J.C.F.	Baroque	D	¢	Continuous 16th note passages; fingerings in broken chord patterns
	108	Minuet in G	Bach (notebook)	Baroque	G	$\frac{3}{4}$	Broken chord arpeggios in both hands; triplets; articulation
	110	Tolling Bell	Heller	Romantic	Bm	$\frac{3}{4}$	Pedal technique; broken chord patterns in both hands; choreography of both hands
	112	Bourrée in E Minor	Bach, J.S.	Baroque	Em	¢	Articulation and phrasing; LH/RH coordination; frequent hand shifts
	114	The Limpid Stream	Burgmüller	Romantic	G	$\frac{4}{4}$	Balance with melody/accompaniment in one hand; LH melody; triplets
	116	The Murmuring Brook	Gurlitt	Romantic	G	$\frac{2}{4}$	Balance with melody/accompaniment in one hand; LH melody; 16th notes
	118	Quiet Morning	Maykapar	Romantic	F	$\frac{12}{8}$	Pedal technique; $\frac{12}{8}$ time signature; balance and beauty of tone
	119	Waltz	Schubert	Romantic	B♭	$\frac{3}{4}$	Vertical reading, B-flat key signature; balance between hands, articulation

Etude
Op. 823, No. 2

Carl Czerny
(1791–1857)

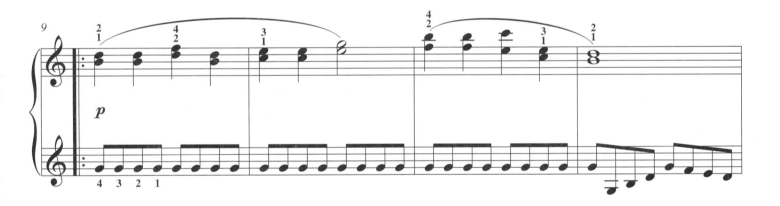

Arabesque
Op. 100, No. 2

Friedrich Burgmüller
(1806-1874)

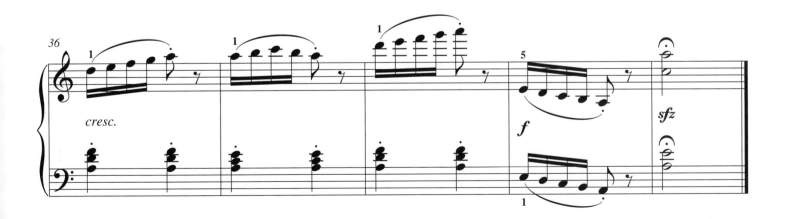

Humming Song
Op. 68, No. 3

Robert Schumann
(1810-1856)

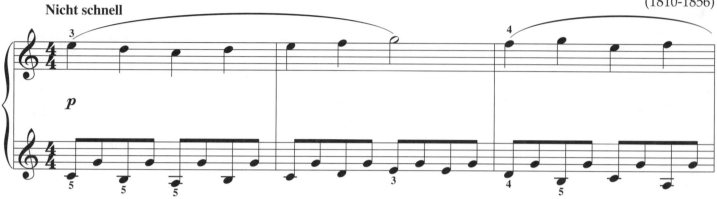

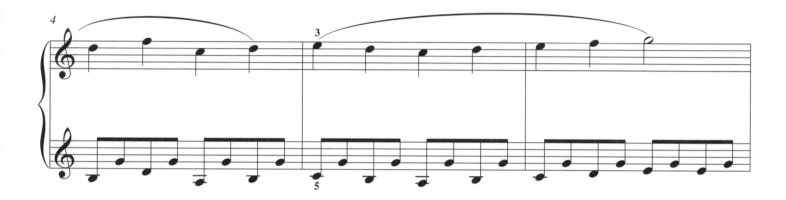

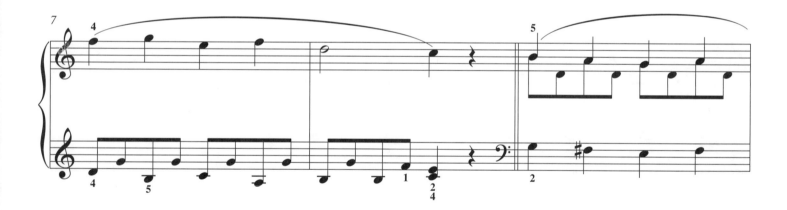

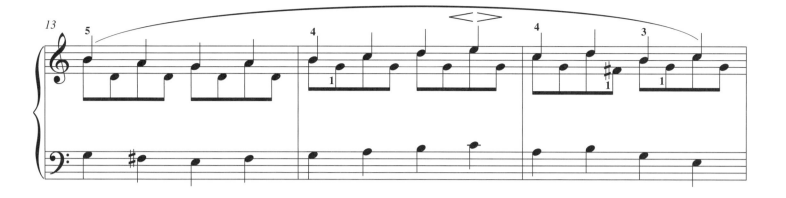

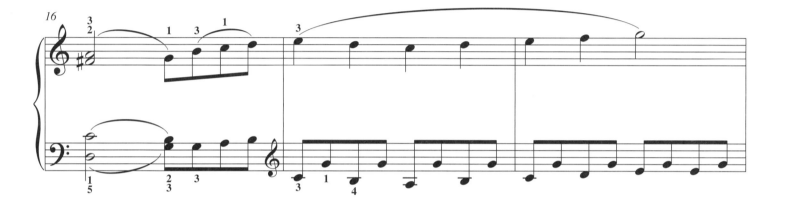

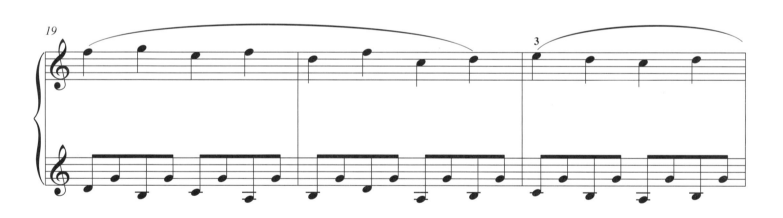

Russian Folk Song
Op. 107, No. 7

Ludwig van Beethoven
(1770-1827)

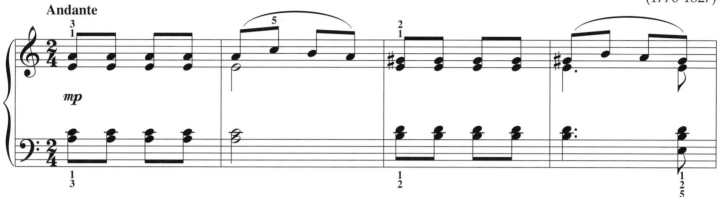

The Bear

Vladimir Rebikoff
(1866-1920)

Andante pesante

Musette

Notebook for Anna Magdalena Bach
18th century

Sonatina in G

Thomas Attwood
(1765-1838)

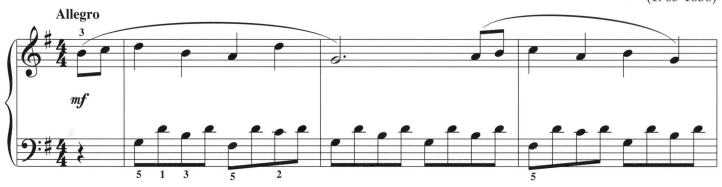

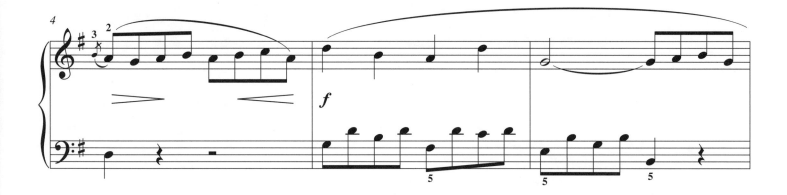

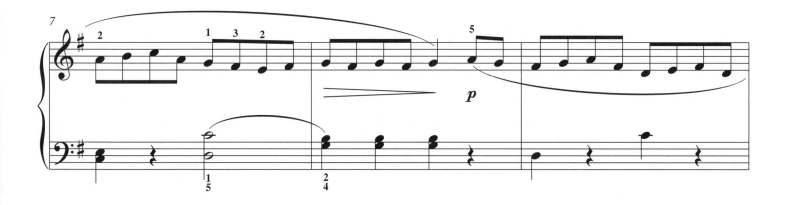

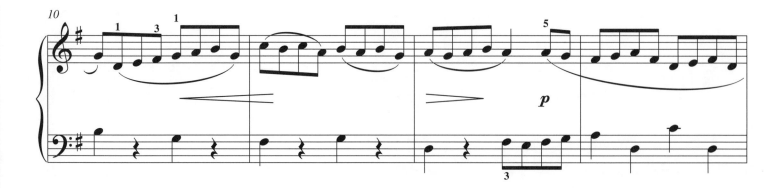

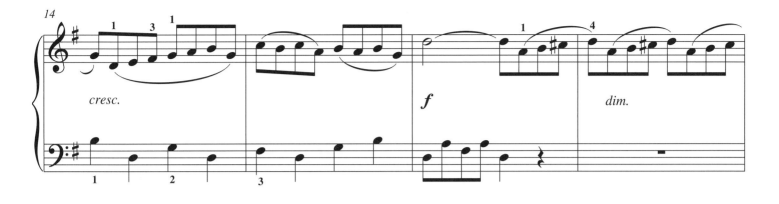

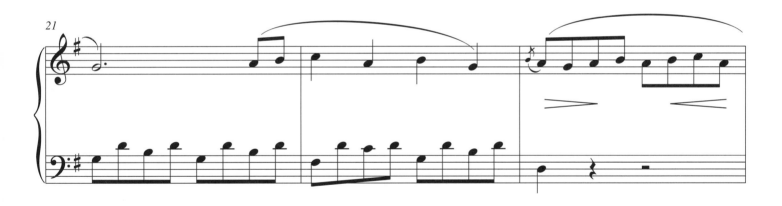

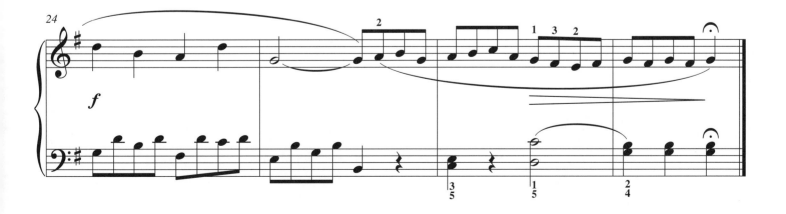

Ecossaise

Ludwig van Beethoven
(1770-1827)

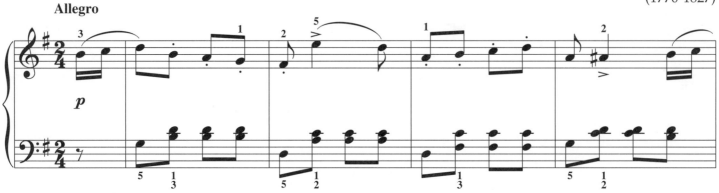

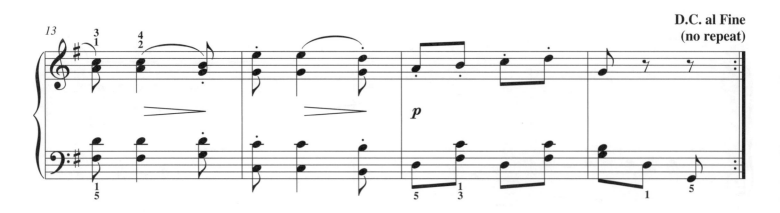

Tarantella
Op. 157, No. 1

Fritz Spindler
(1817-1905)

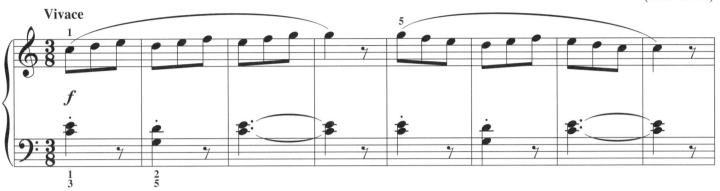

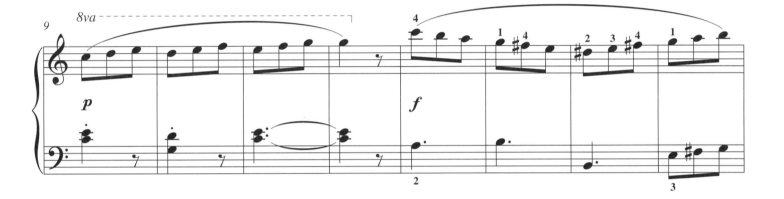

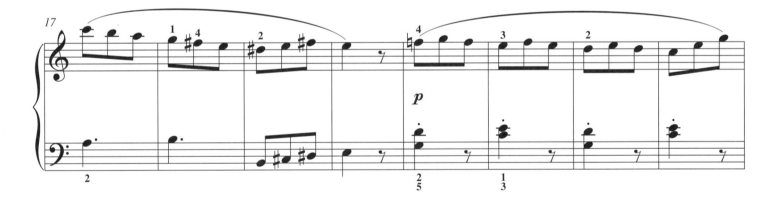

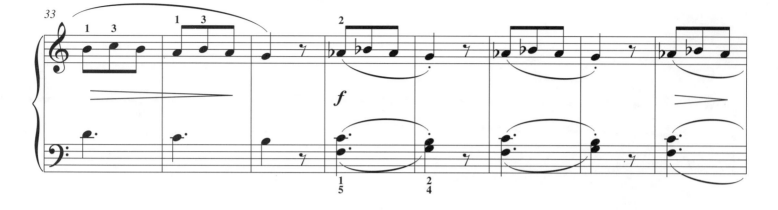

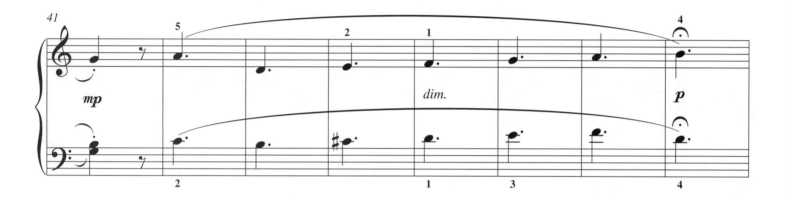

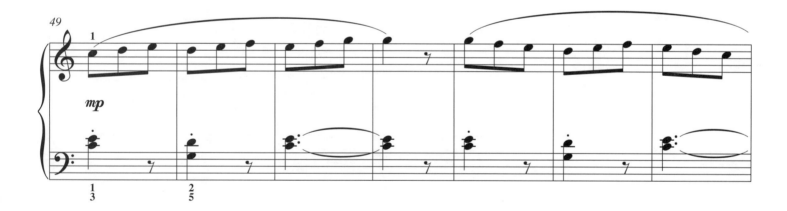

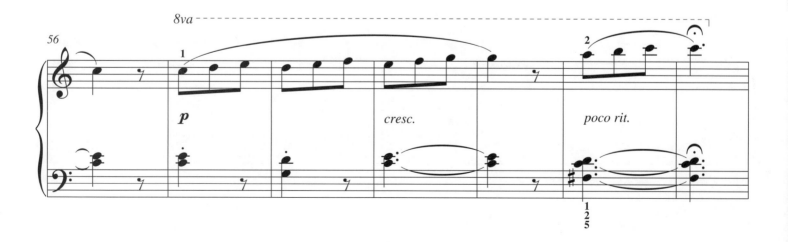

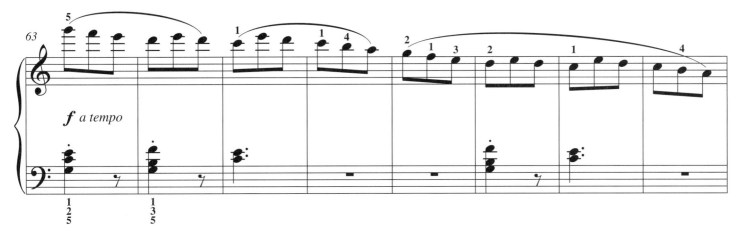

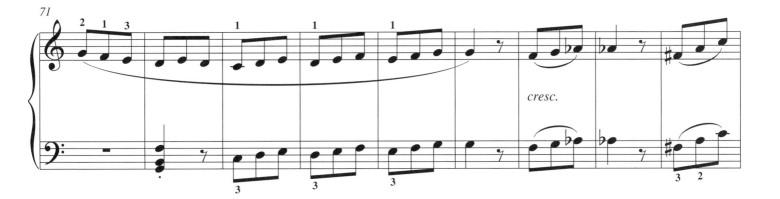

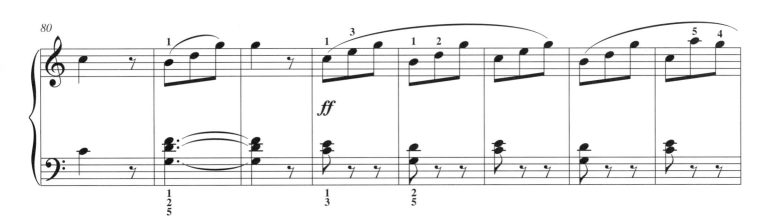

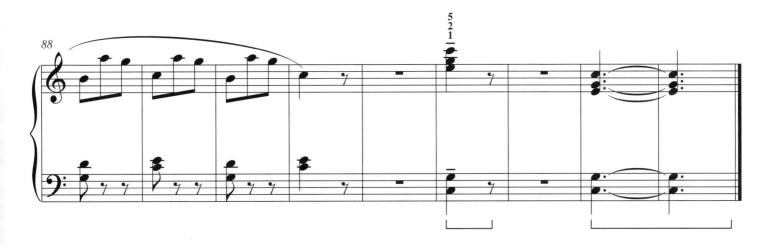

Russian Polka

Michael Ivanovich Glinka
(1804-1857)

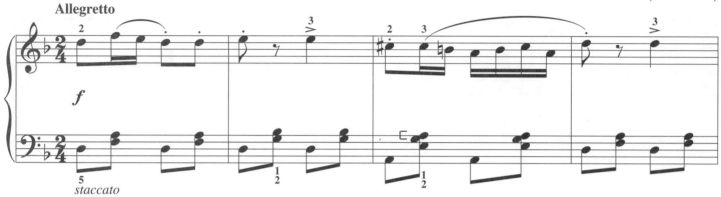

Spanish Dance
Op. 61, No. 10

Theodor Oesten
(1813-1870)

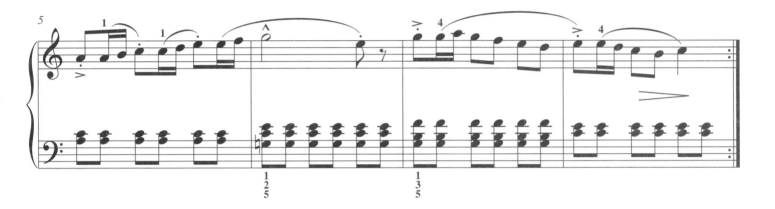

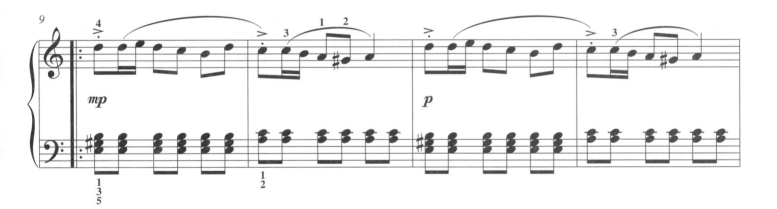

Sonatina in C

Jean T. Latour
(1766-1837)

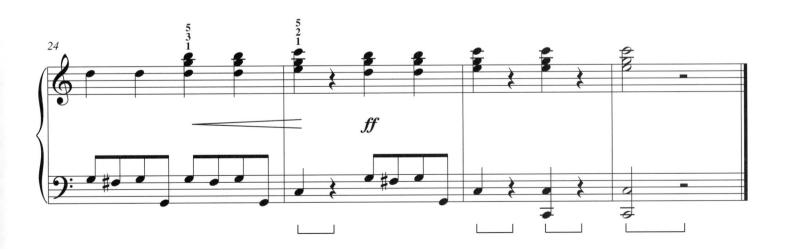

Wild Rider
Op. 68, No. 8

Robert Schumann
(1810-1856)

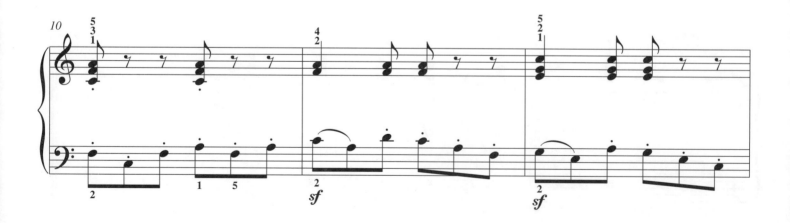

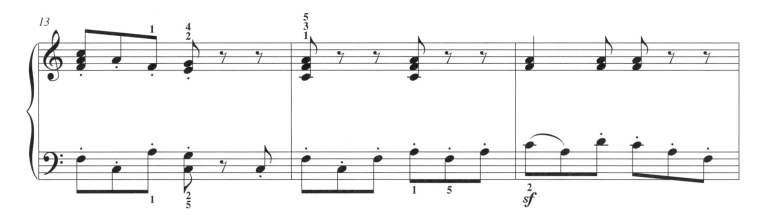

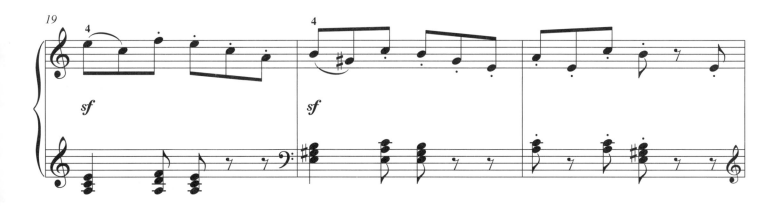

Theme and Variation
Op. 228

Cornelius Gurlitt
(1820-1901)

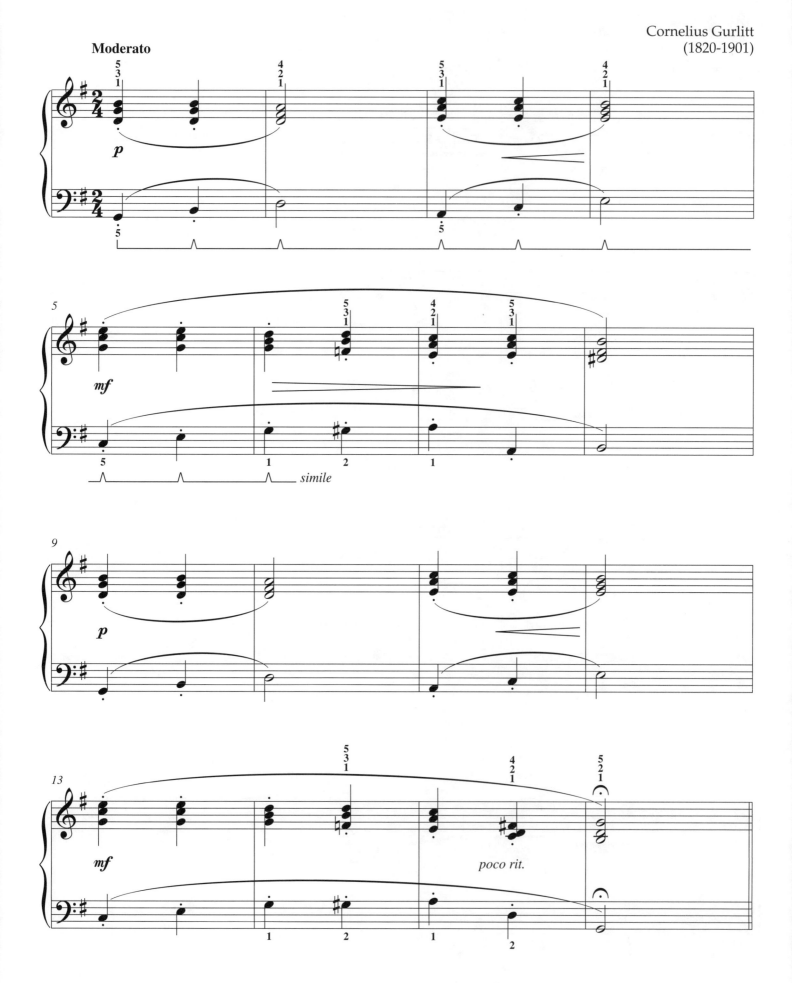

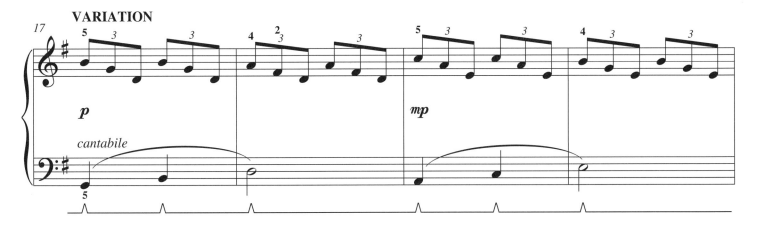

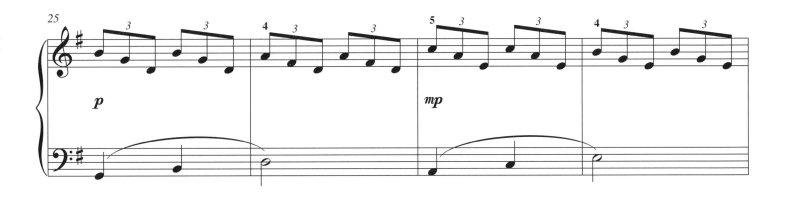

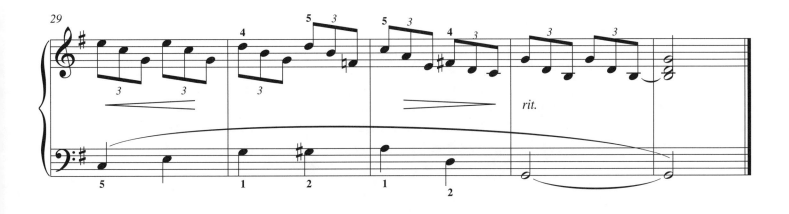

Sonatina in C

I

Muzio Clementi
(1752-1832)

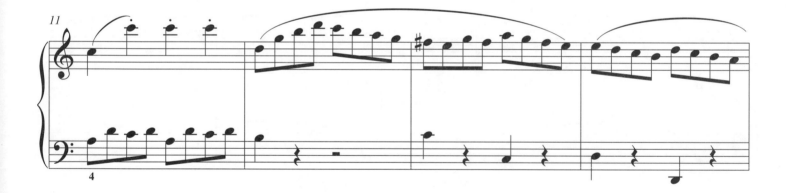

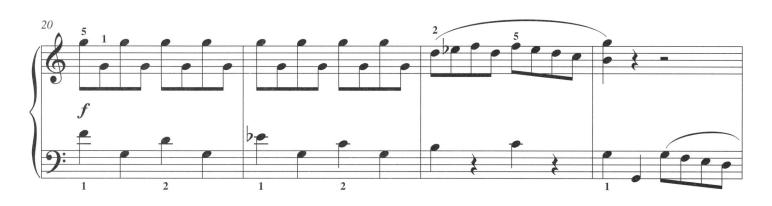

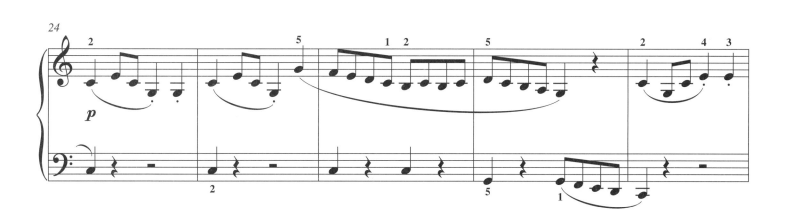

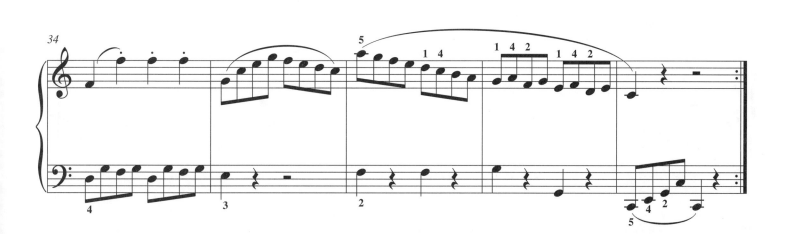

Minuet and Trio

Wolfgang Amadeus Mozart
(1756-1791)

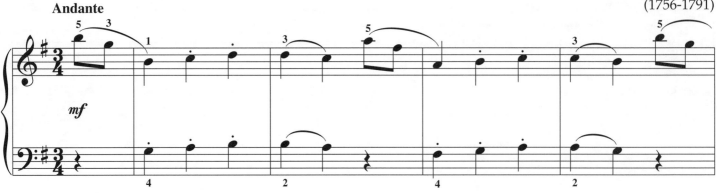

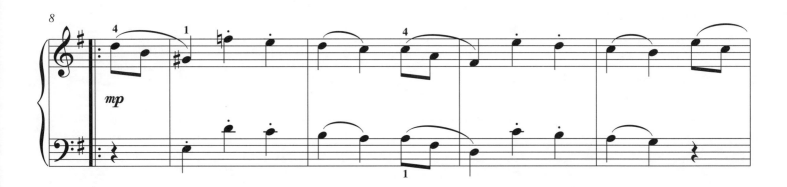

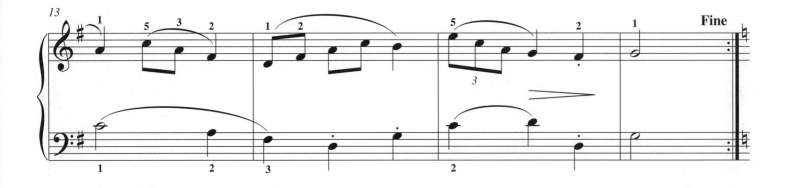

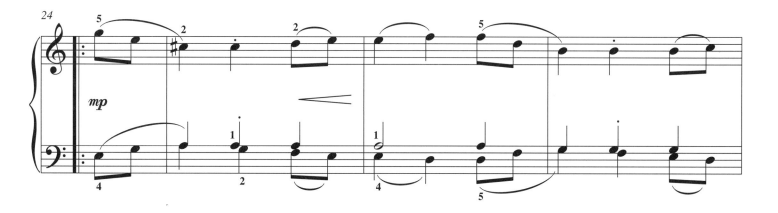

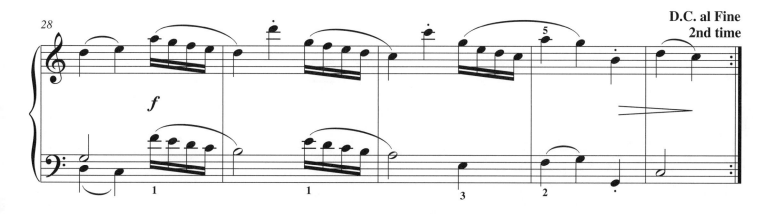

Menuet in D Minor

Notebook for Anna Magdalena Bach
18th century

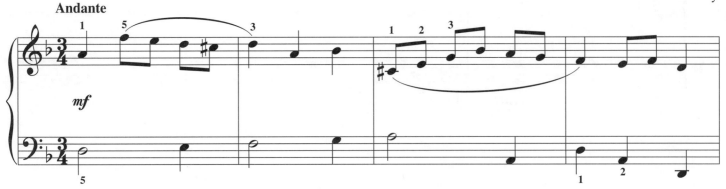

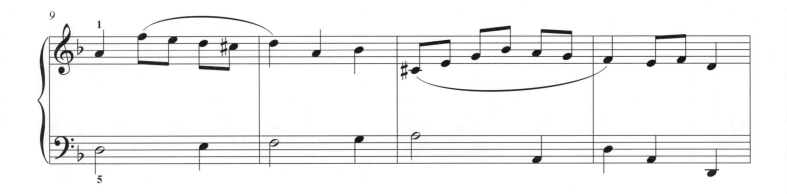

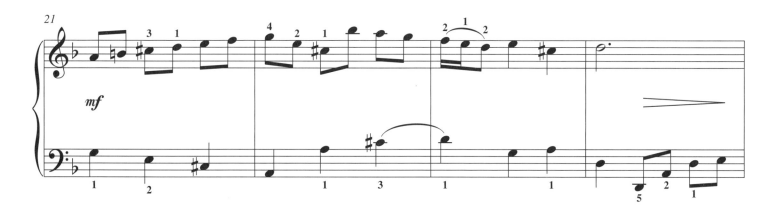

Solfeggio

Johann Christoph Friedrich Bach
(1732-1795)

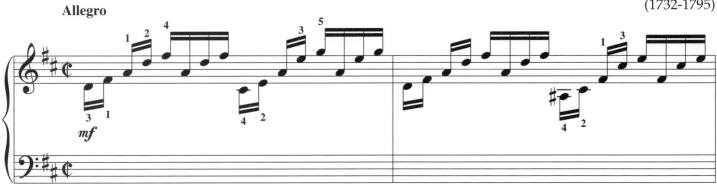

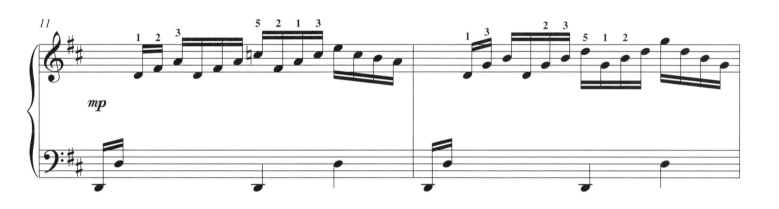

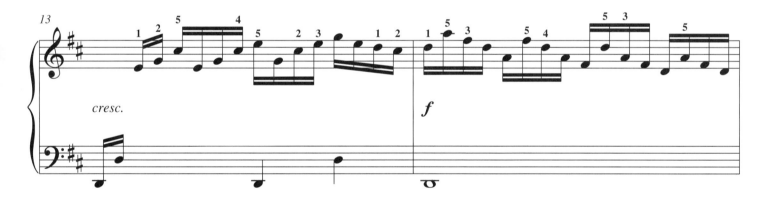

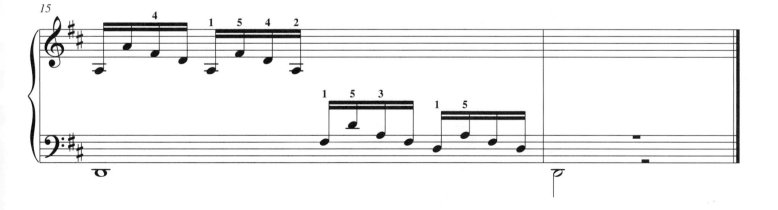

Minuet in G

Notebook for Anna Magdalena Bach
18th century

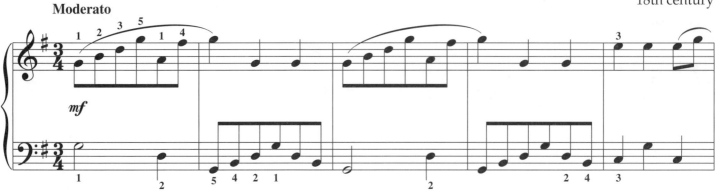

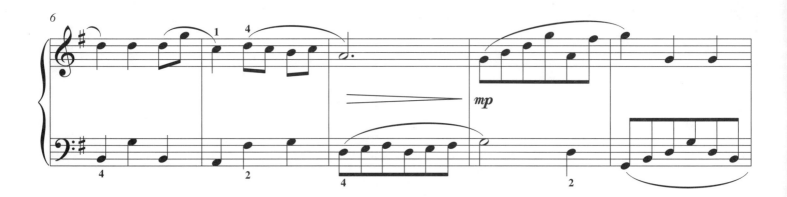

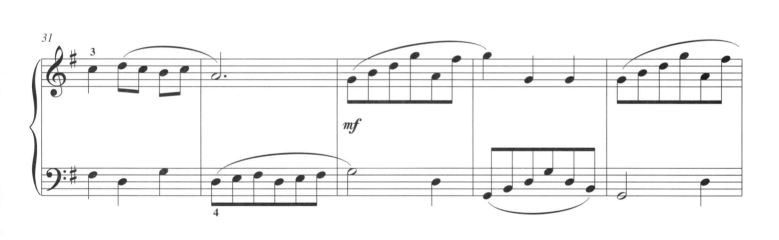

Tolling Bell

Op. 125, No. 8

Stephen Heller
(1813-1888)

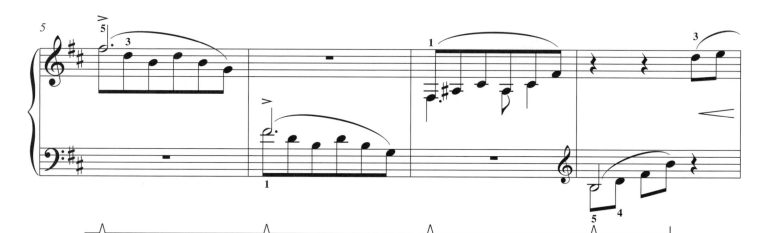

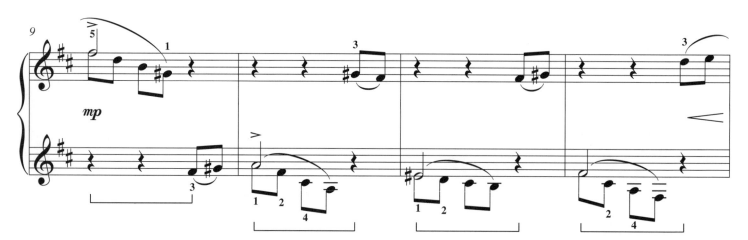

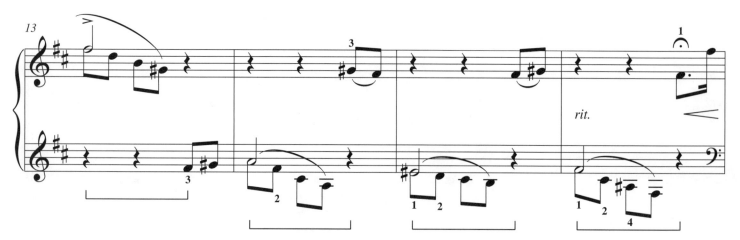

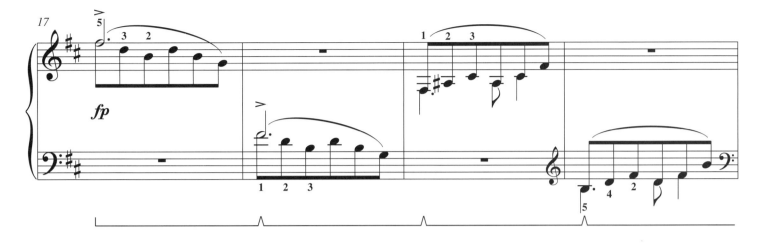

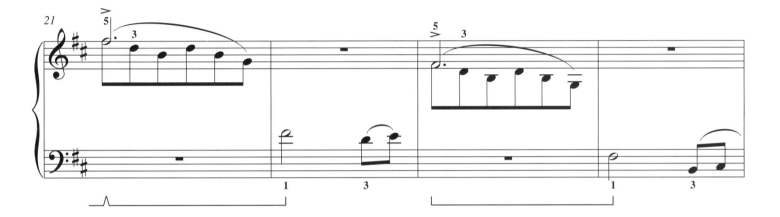

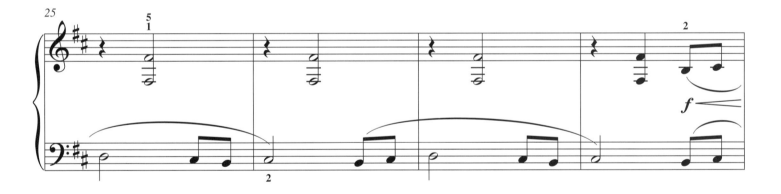

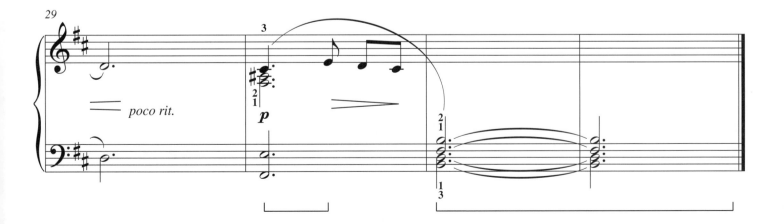

Bourrée in E Minor
BWV 996

Johann Sebastian Bach
(1685-1750)

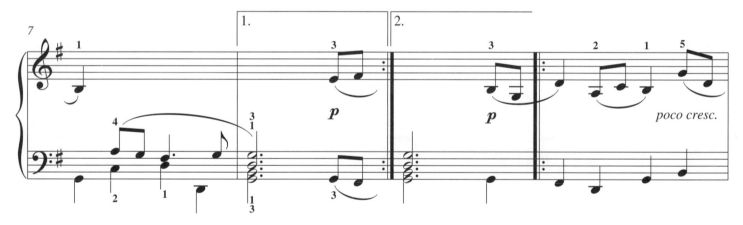

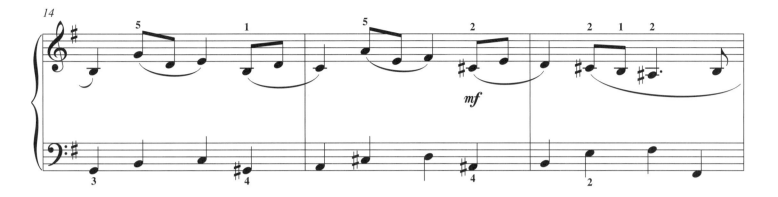

The Limpid Stream

Op. 100, No. 7

Friedrich Burgmüller
(1806-1874)

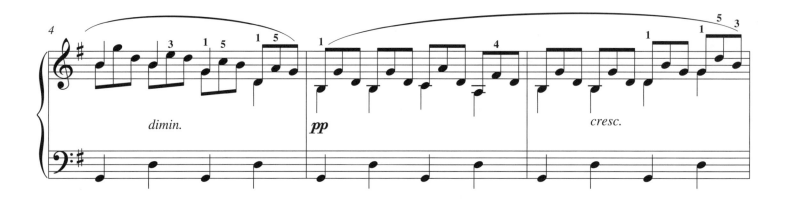

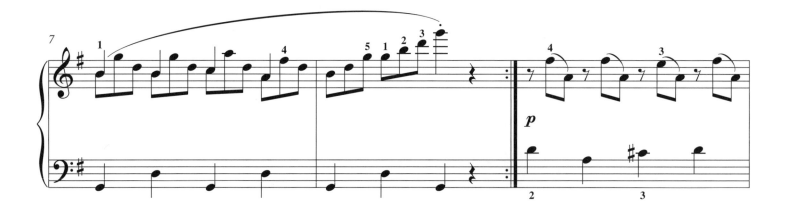

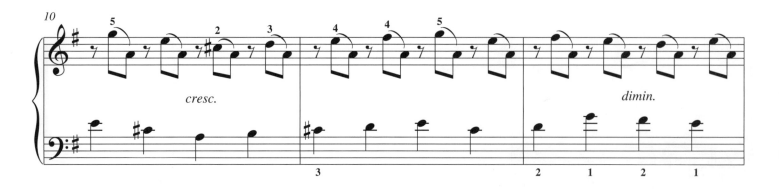

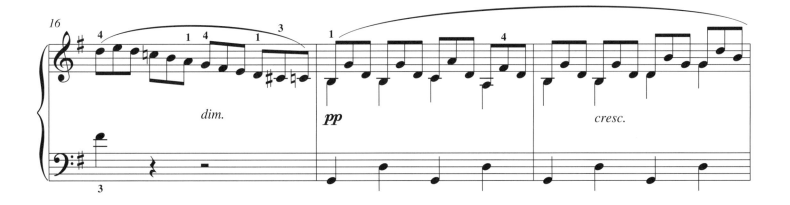

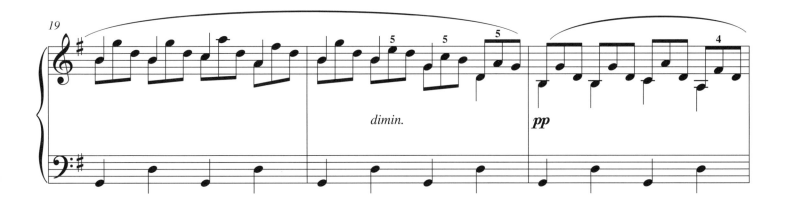

The Murmuring Brook
Op. 140, No. 5

Cornelius Gurlitt
(1820-1901)

Quiet Morning

Samuel Maykapar
(1867-1938)

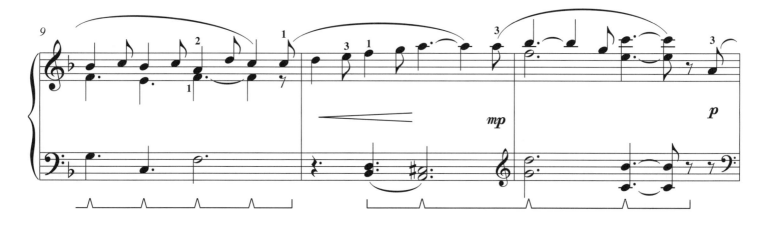

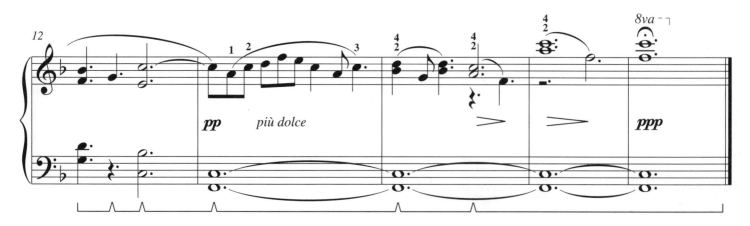

Waltz
Op. 127, No. 15

Franz Schubert
(1797-1828)

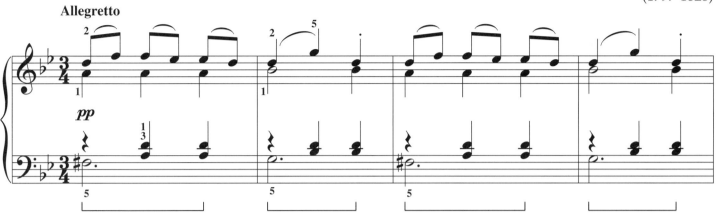

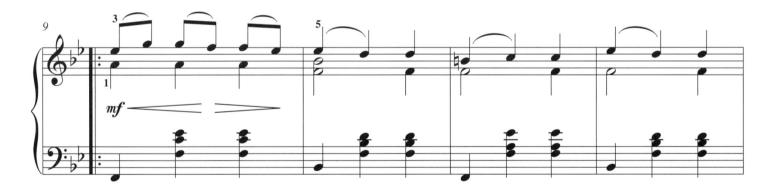

JOURNEY THROUGH THE
CLASSICS

BOOK 4
Intermediate

BOOK 4 · INTERMEDIATE
Reference Chart

✔ WHEN COMPLETED	PAGE	TITLE	COMPOSER	ERA	KEY	METER	CHALLENGE ELEMENTS
	122	Little Prelude	Bach, J.S.	Baroque	C	4/4	Expanded hand position in broken chords; ornaments
	123	Mazurka	Gurlitt	Romantic	C	3/4	Dotted rhythms; chromatic scale
	124	Minuet	Mozart, W.A.	Classical	F	3/4	Triplet and 16th note patterns; ornaments
	126	Intrada	Graupner	Baroque	C	4/4	Shifting octaves in the LH; Rotation and LH/RH coordination
	128	Sonatina in G	Beethoven	Classical	G	4/4	Articulation; Alberti bass and balance between hands
	132	Spinning Song	Ellmenreich	Romantic	F	2/4	Legato/staccato coordination between hands; 16th notes and syncopation
	136	Old French Song	Tchaikovsky	Romantic	Gm	2/4	Cantabile tone with careful legato fingering; legato/staccato coordination
	138	Gavotte in A Minor	Pachelbel	Baroque	Am	4/4	Articulation and ornaments; dynamic contrasts
	138	Gavotte and Variation	Pachelbel	Baroque	Am	4/4	Dotted rhythms; articulation and ornaments; 16th note passages
	140	The Merry Farmer	Schumann	Romantic	F	4/4	LH melody; voicing and balance between hands
	141	Sonatina in A Minor	Benda	Classical	Am	2/4	Shared LH/RH 16th note patterns; syncopation and articulation
	144	Waltz in A Minor	Chopin	Romantic	Am	3/4	Waltz bass; balance between hands; pedaling and ornaments
	147	Sonatina Op. 36, No. 2 (III)	Clementi	Classical	G	3/8	Legato/staccato coordination between hands; 16th note passages; trill
	152	Invention No. 1	Bach, J.S.	Baroque	C	4/4	Coordination of contrapuntal elements and ornaments
	154	By the Spring	Gurlitt	Romantic	A	2/4	A major key signature; careful pedal technique and balance between hands
	156	The Avalanche	Heller	Romantic	Am	2/4	Vertical reading and rolled chords; quick scale passages divided between hands
	159	Little Prelude in C Minor	Bach, J.S.	Baroque	Cm	3/4	Continuous 16th note passages; fingerings in broken chord patterns
	162	Sonatina Op. 55, No. 1 (I)	Kuhlau	Classical	C	4/4	Scale passages and Alberti bass; balance between melody and accompaniment
	166	From Foreign Lands and People	Schumann	Romantic	G	2/4	Voicing of melody; coordination of accompaniment; dotted versus triplet rhythms
	167	The Storm	Burgmüller	Romantic	Dm	4/4	Both hands in bass; rotation of broken octaves; voicing of melody in LH
	170	German Dance	Schubert	Romantic	Am	3/4	Careful pedaling; ornaments, voicing, legato octaves in melody
	172	Solfeggietto	Bach, C.P.E.	Baroque	Cm	4/4	Even touch tone; coordinating continuous 16th notes shared between hands
	176	To a Wild Rose	MacDowell	Romantic	A	2/4	A major key signature; voicing of melody; phrasing and pedaling
	178	Für Elise	Beethoven	Classical	Am	3/8	Voicing and balance; pedal technique; 64th notes; repeated notes; chromatic scale

Little Prelude
BWV 939

Johann Sebastian Bach
(1685–1750)

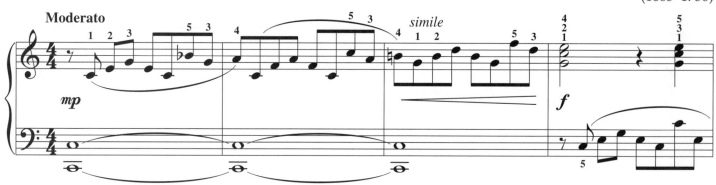

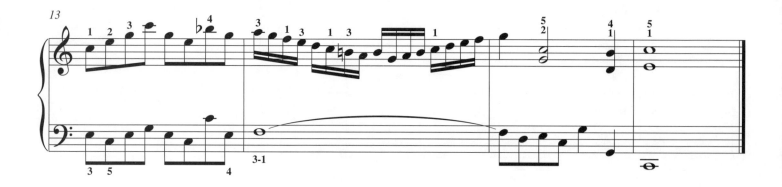

Mazurka

Cornelius Gurlitt
(1820–1901)

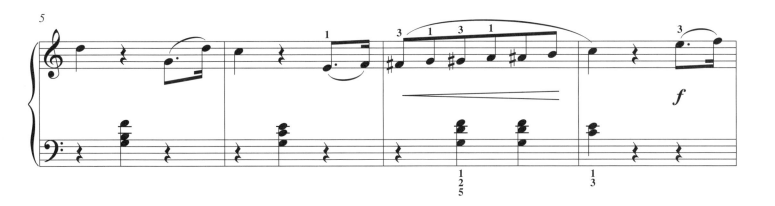

Minuet
KV 5

Wolfgang Amadeus Mozart
(1756–1791)

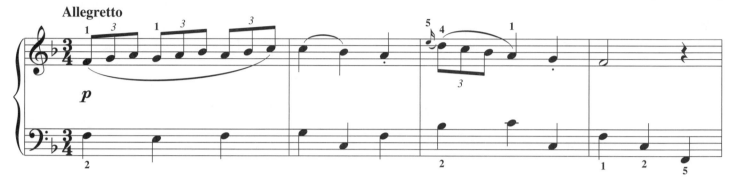

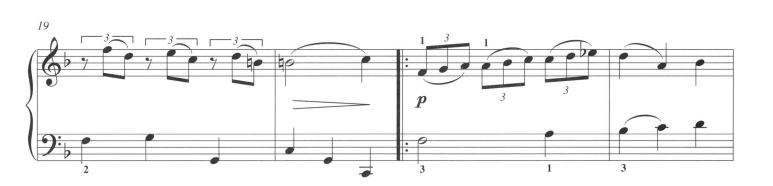

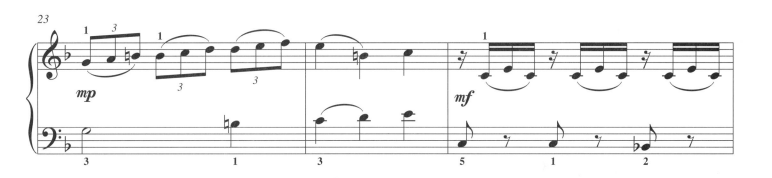

Intrada

Christoph Graupner
(1683–1760)

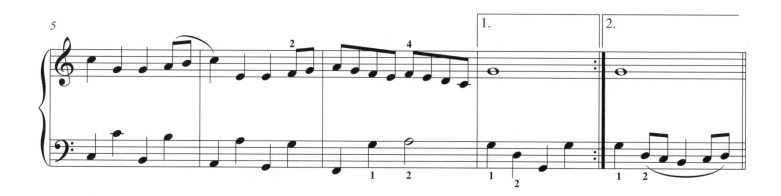

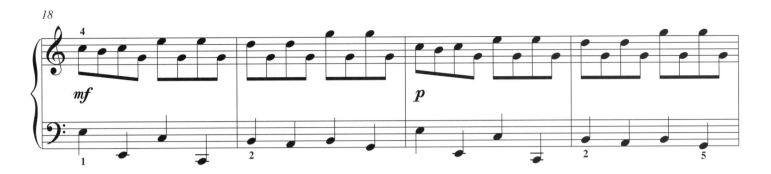

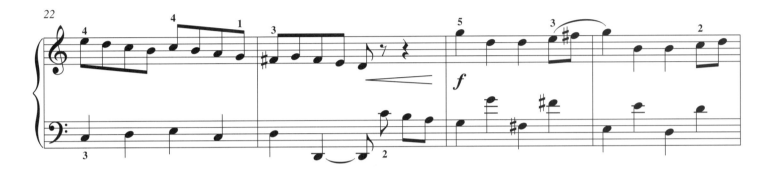

Sonatina in G

Ludwig van Beethoven
(1770–1827)

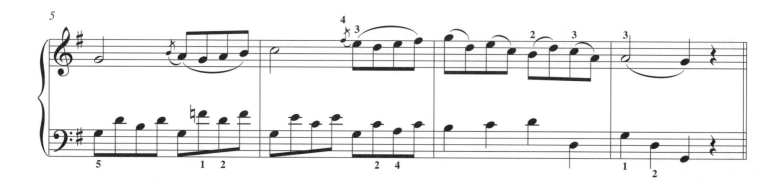

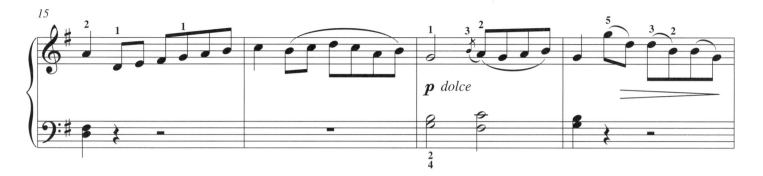

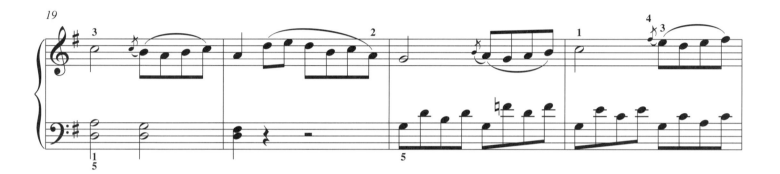

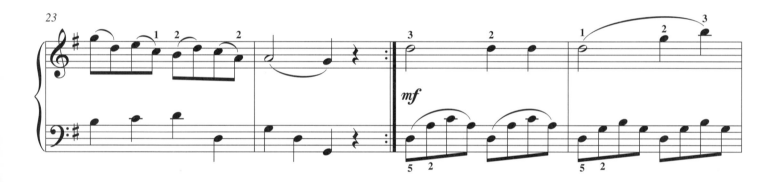

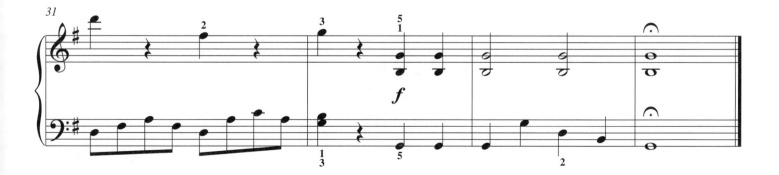

Romanze

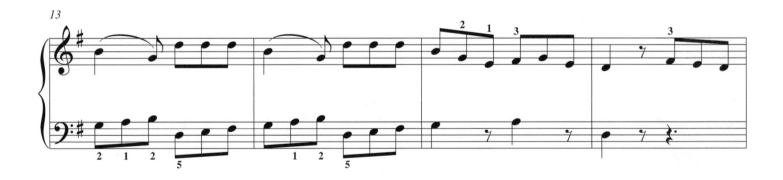

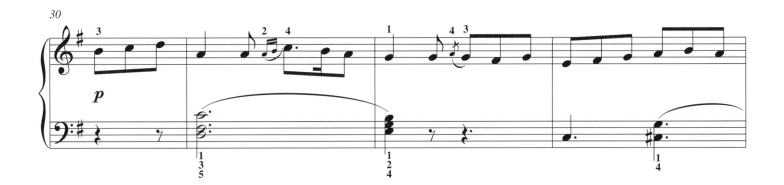

Spinning Song

Albert Ellmenreich
(1816–1905)

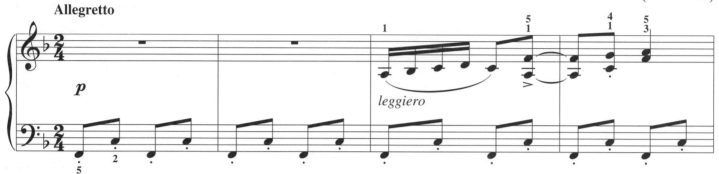

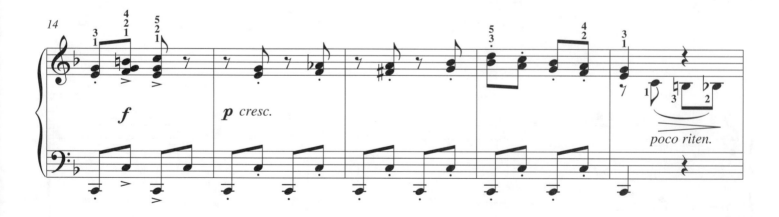

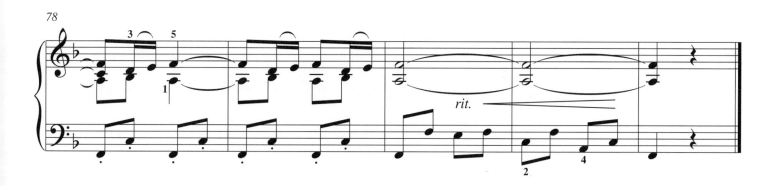

Old French Song
Op. 39, No. 16

Pyotr Ilyich Tchaikovsky
(1840–1893)

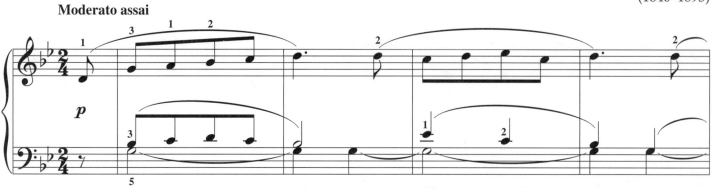

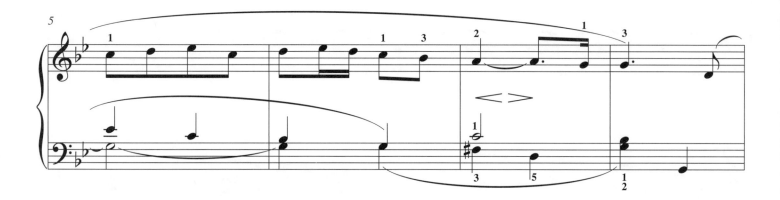

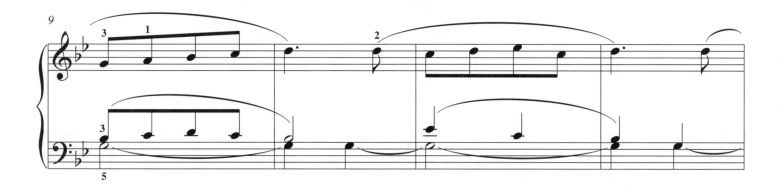

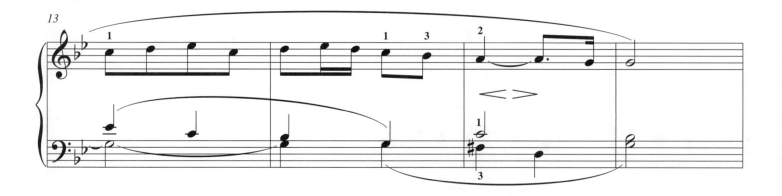

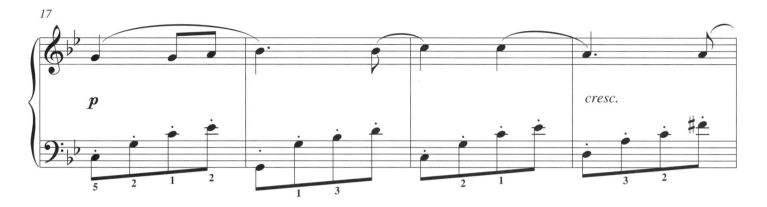

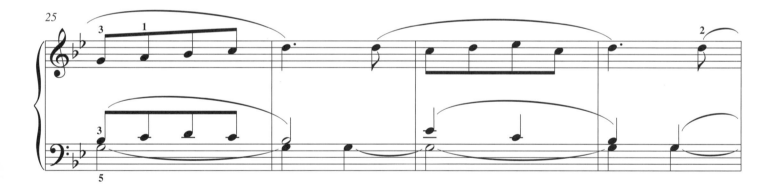

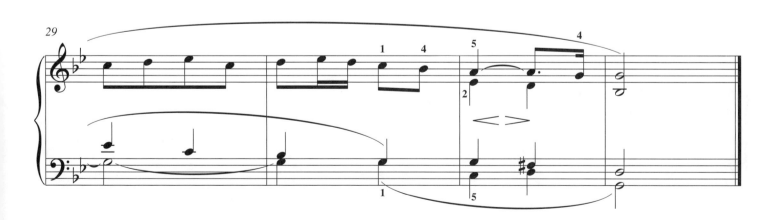

Gavotte in A Minor

Johann Pachelbel
(1653–1706)

Gavotte and Variation

Johann Pachelbel
(1653–1706)

Variation

The Merry Farmer
Op. 68, No. 10

Robert Schumann
(1810–1856)

Brisk and lively

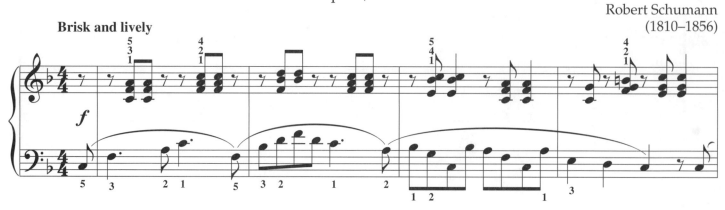

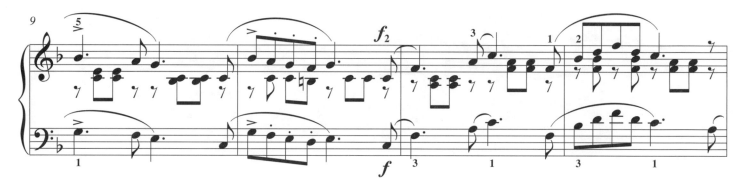

Sonatina in A Minor

Georg Anton Benda
(1722–1795)

Allegro

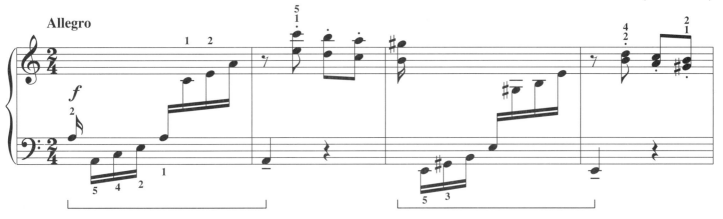

142

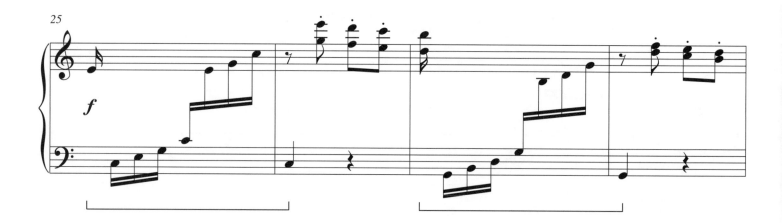

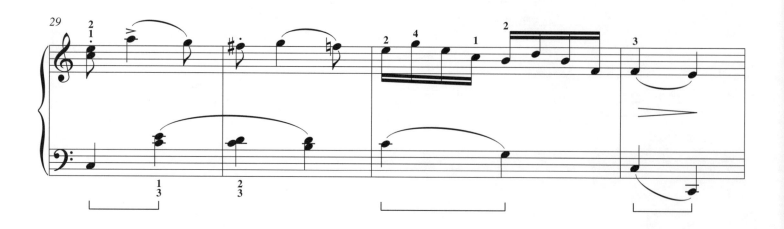

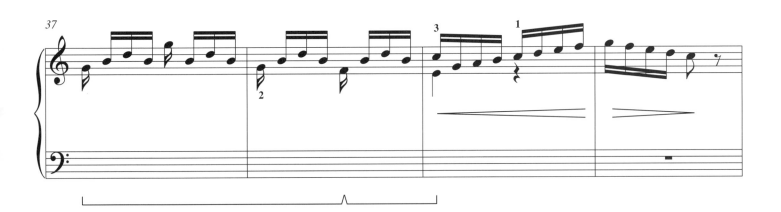

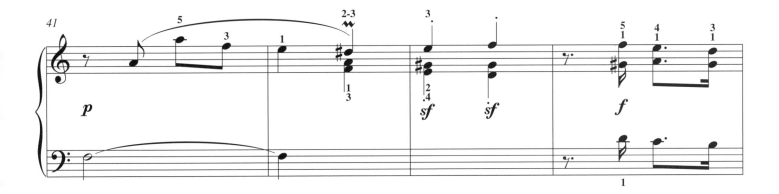

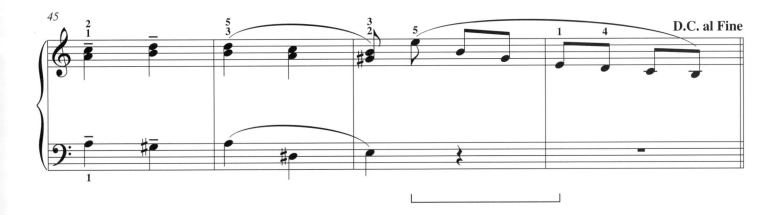

D.C. al Fine

Waltz in A Minor
(Posthumous)

Frédéric Chopin
(1810–1849)

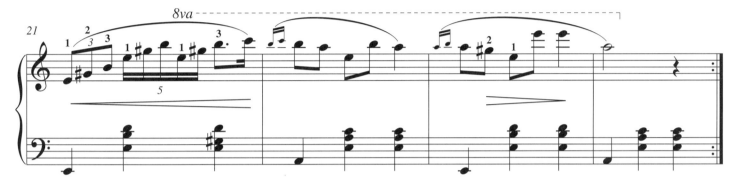

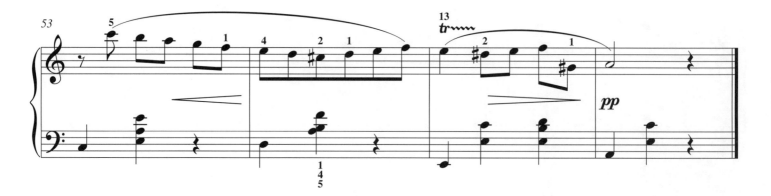

Sonatina
Op. 36, No. 2

III

Muzio Clementi
(1752–1832)

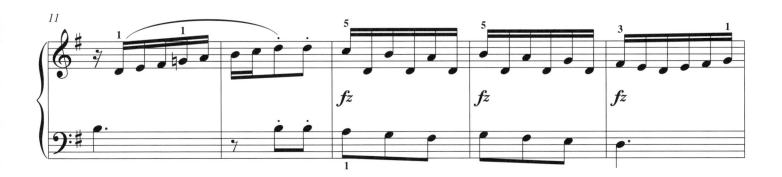

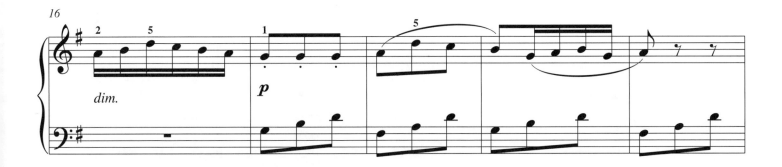

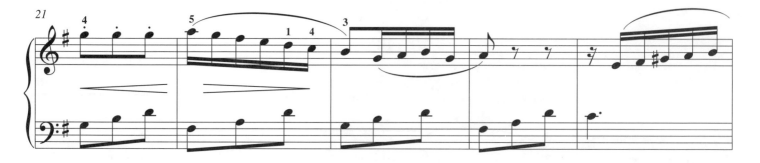

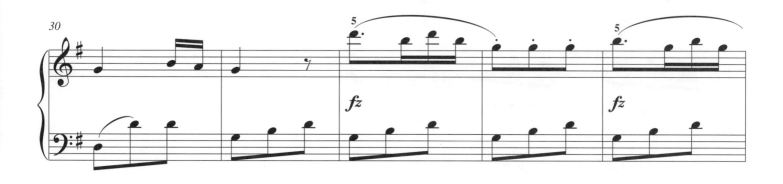

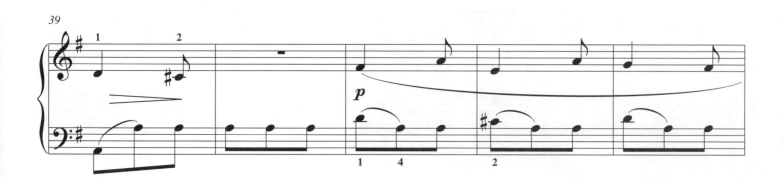

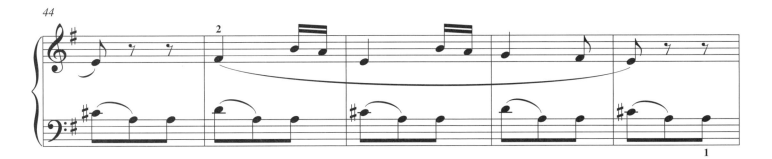

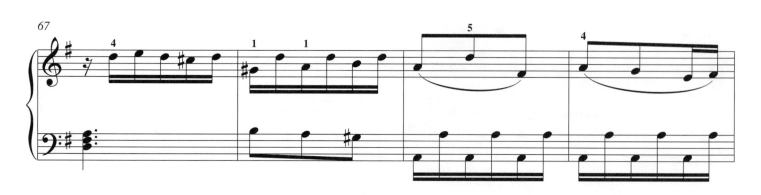

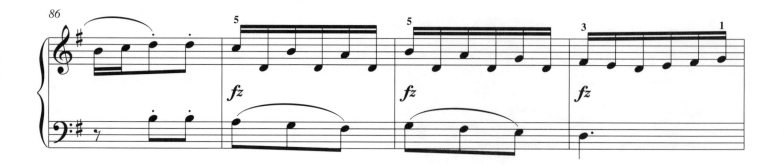

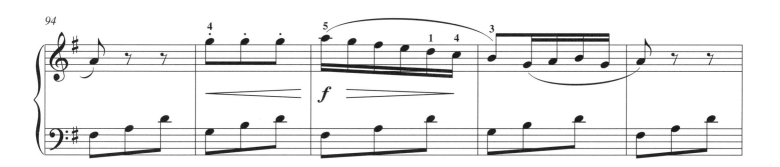

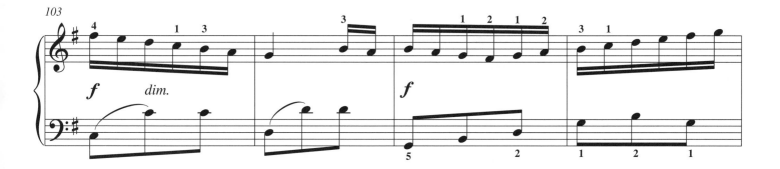

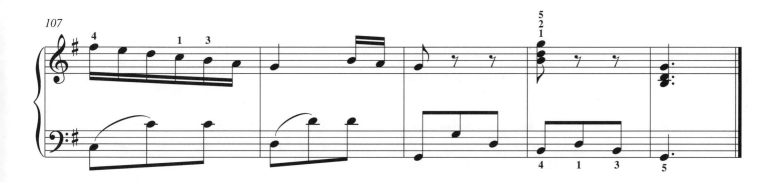

Invention No. 1

Johann Sebastian Bach
(1685-1750)

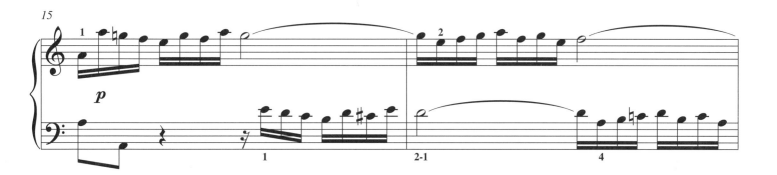

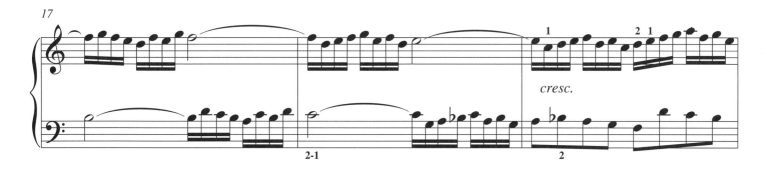

By the Spring
Op. 101, No. 5

Cornelius Gurlitt
(1820-1901)

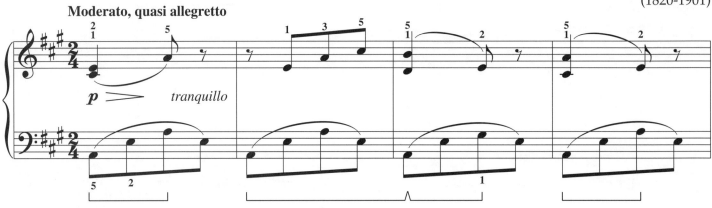

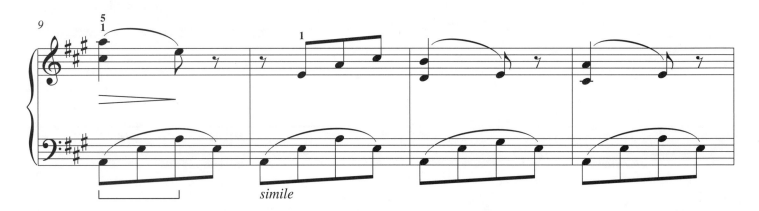

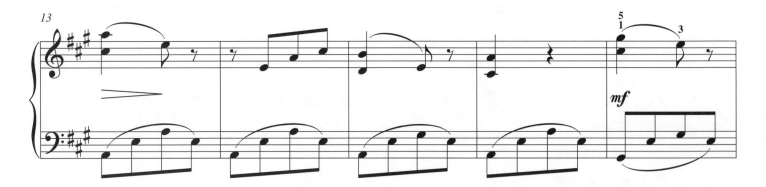

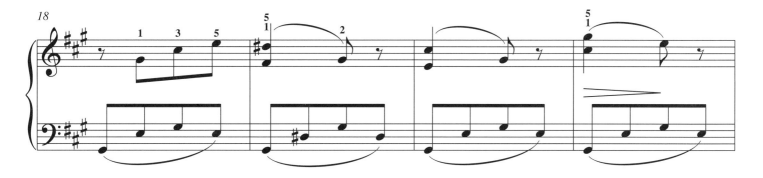

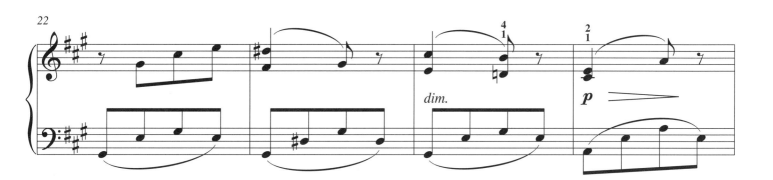

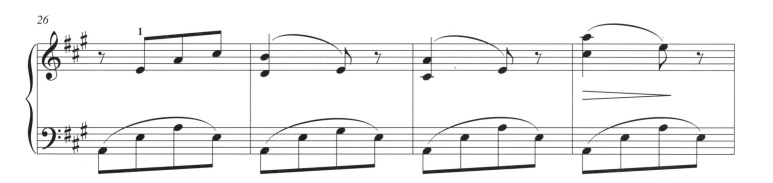

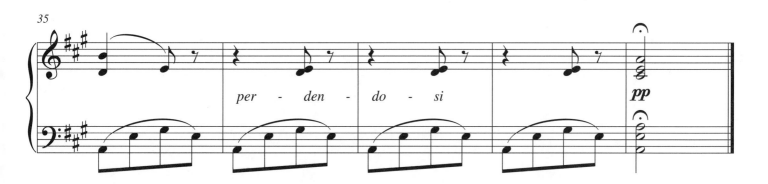

per - den - do - si

The Avalanche
Op. 45, No. 2

Stephen Heller
(1813–1888)

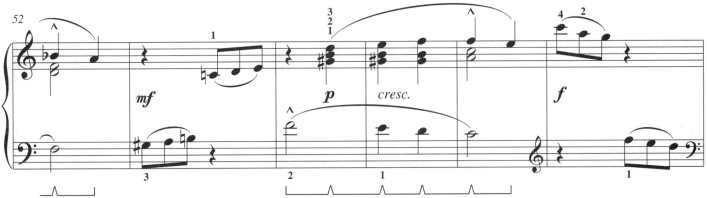

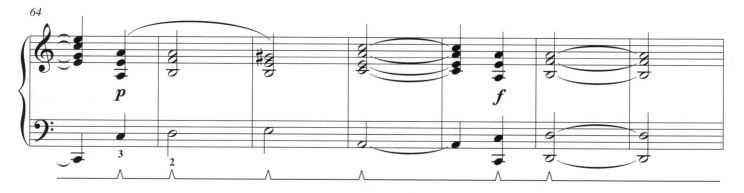

Little Prelude in C Minor
BWV 999

Johann Sebastian Bach
(1685–1750)

Con moto

simile

dim.

Sonatina in C
Op. 55, No. 1

I

Friedrich Kuhlau
(1786–1832)

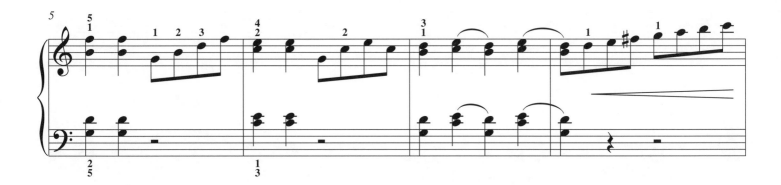

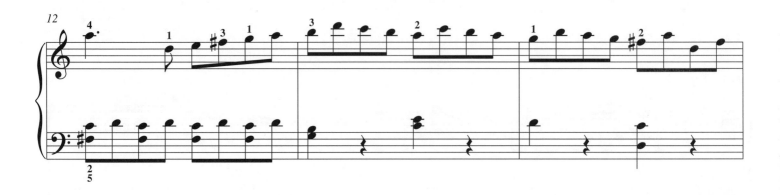

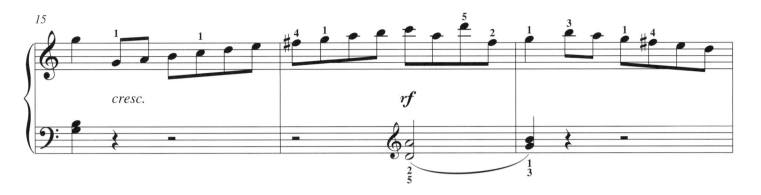

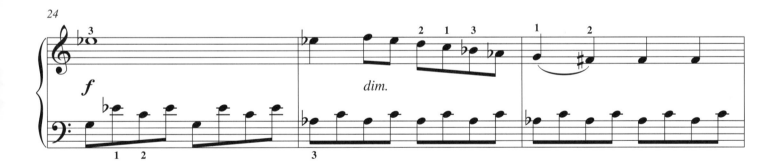

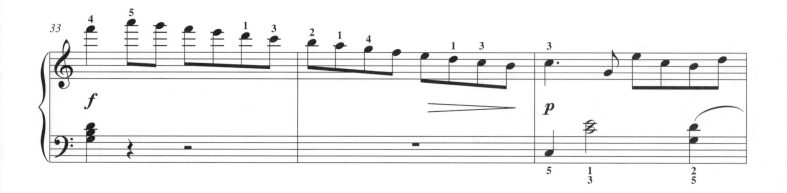

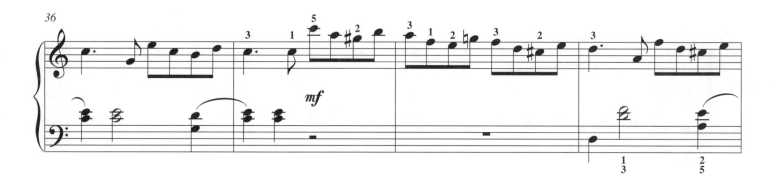

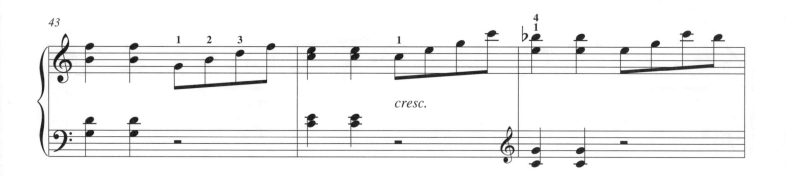

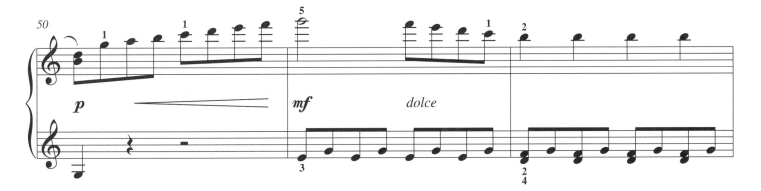

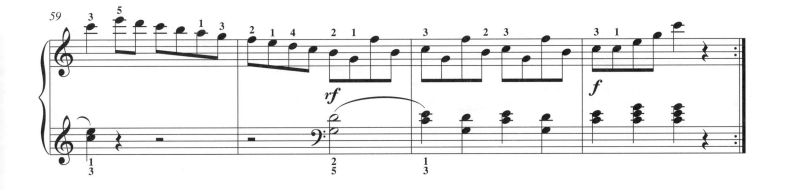

From Foreign Lands and People
Op. 15, No. 1

Robert Schumann
(1810–1856)

Andante

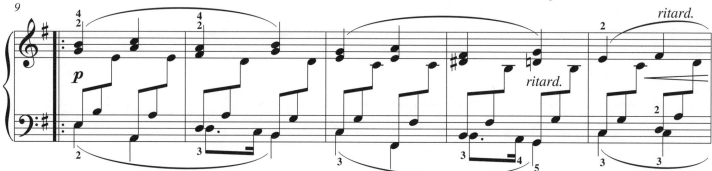

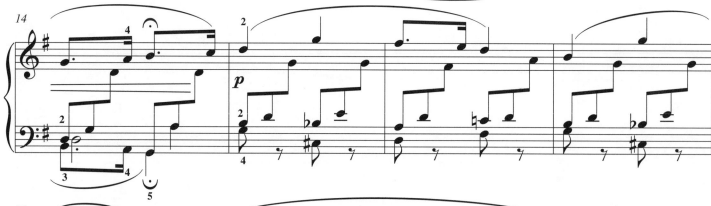

The Storm
Op. 109, No. 13

Friedrich Burgmüller
(1806–1874)

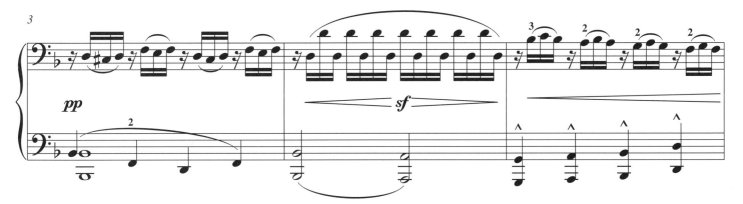

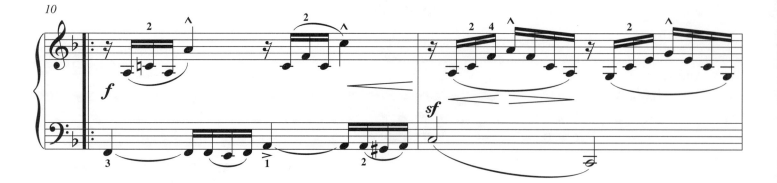

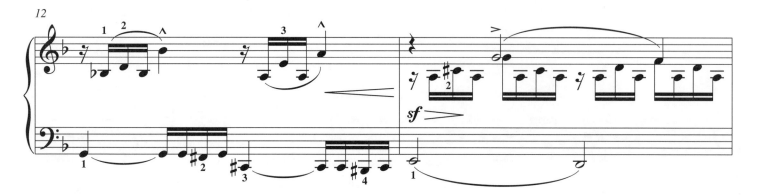

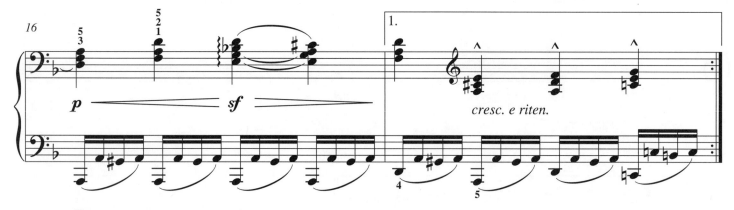

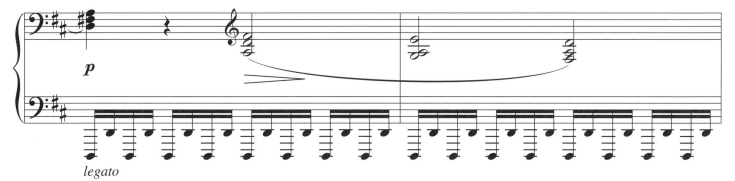

a tempo ma un poco più lento

legato

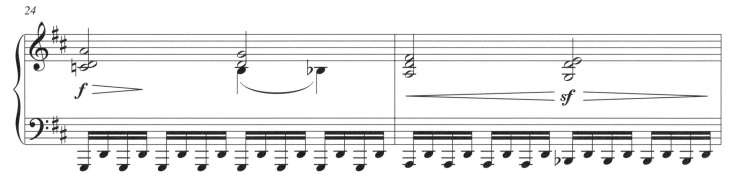

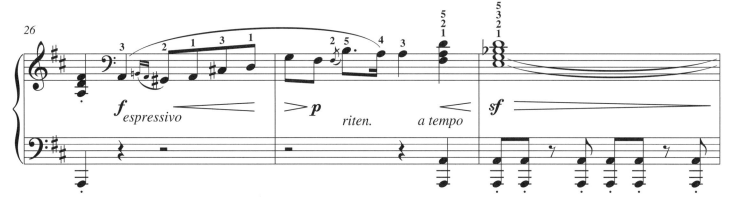

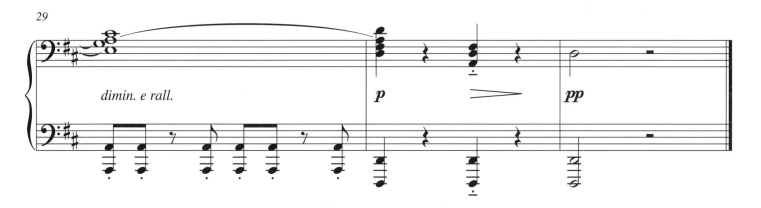

German Dance
Op. 33, No. 10

Franz Schubert
(1797–1828)

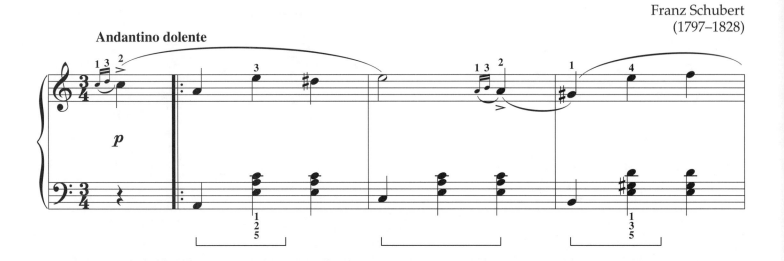

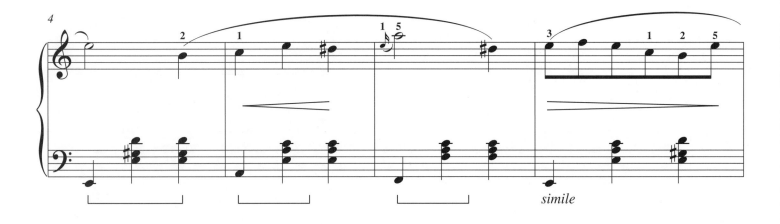

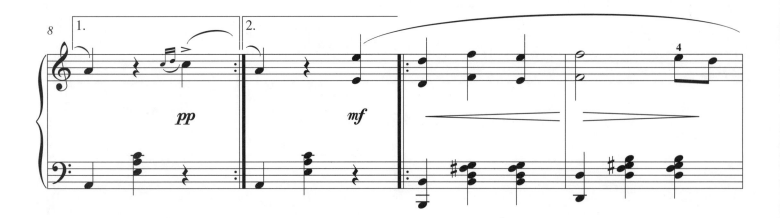

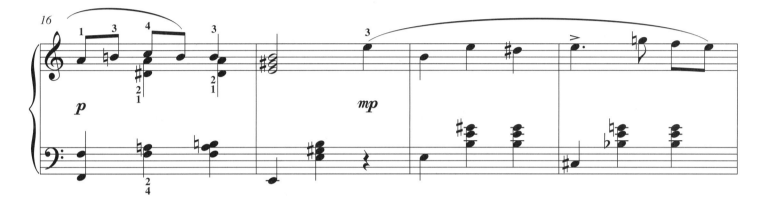

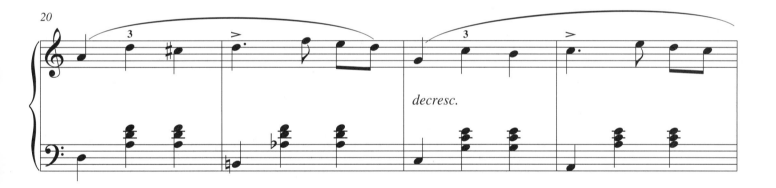

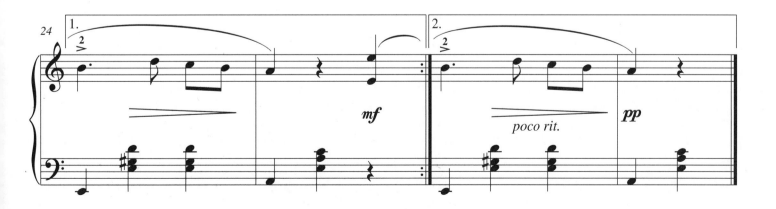

Solfeggietto

Carl Philipp Emanuel Bach
(1714–1788)

Allegro

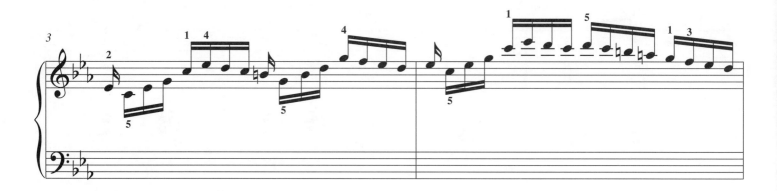

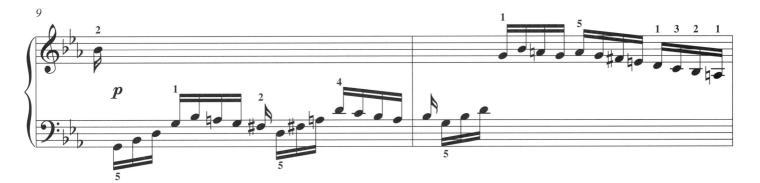

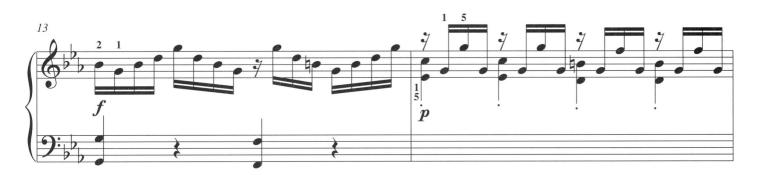

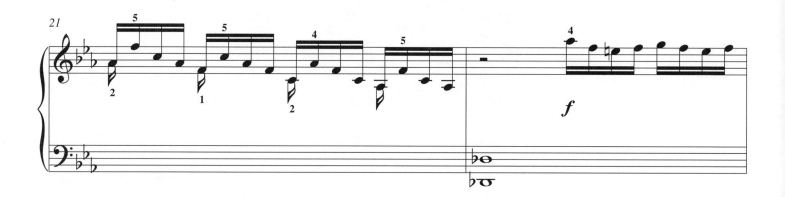

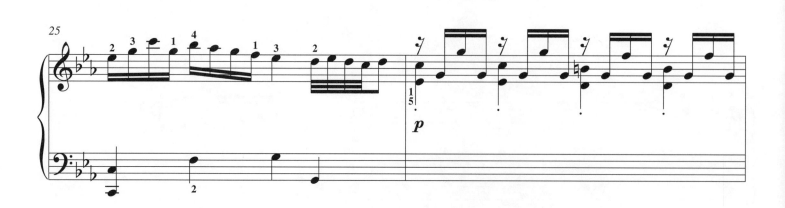

To a Wild Rose
Op. 51, No. 1

Edward MacDowell
(1861–1908)

With simple tenderness

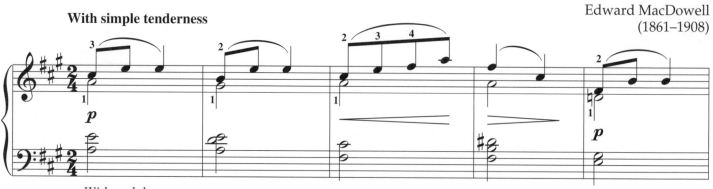

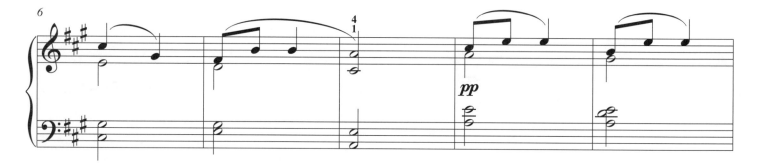

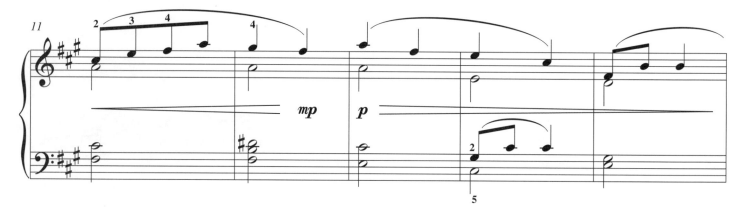

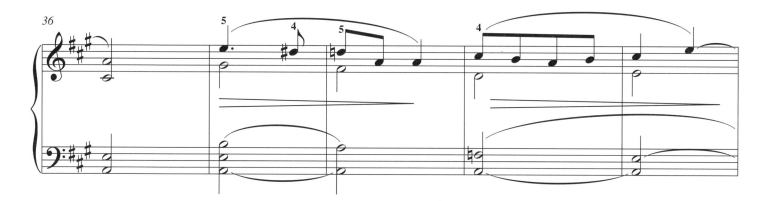

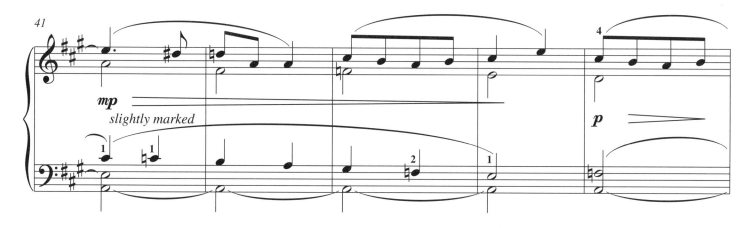

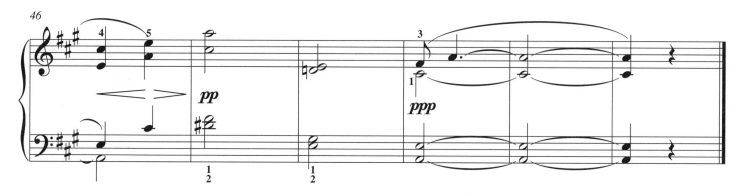

Für Elise
WoO 59

Ludwig van Beethoven
(1770-1827)

Poco moto (molto gracioso)

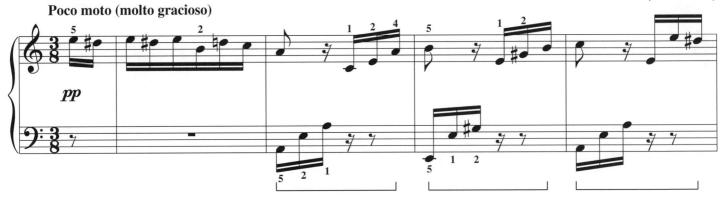

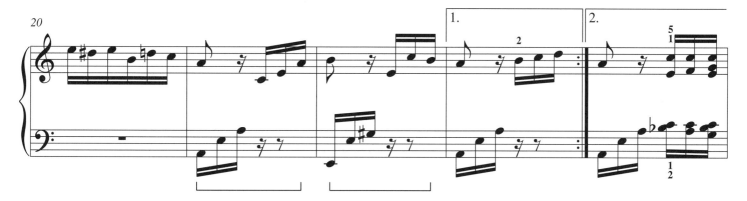

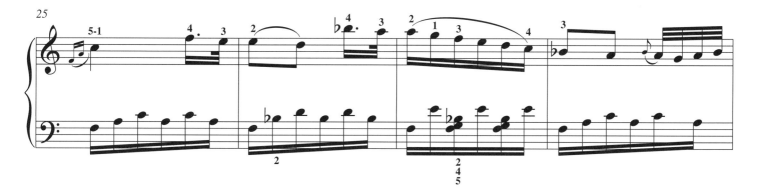

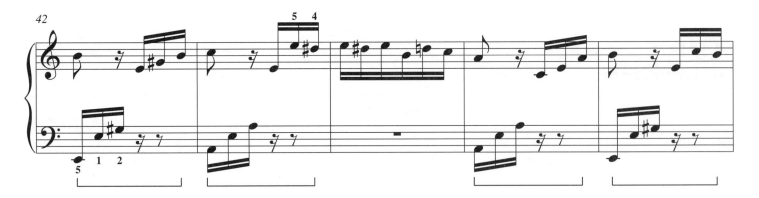

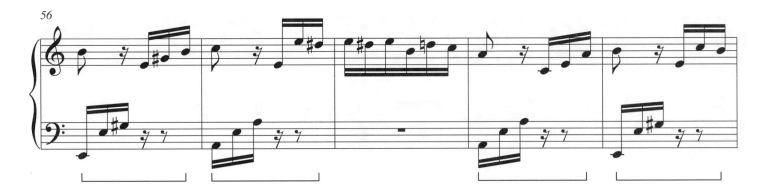

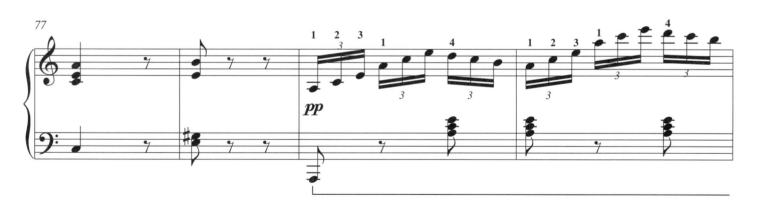

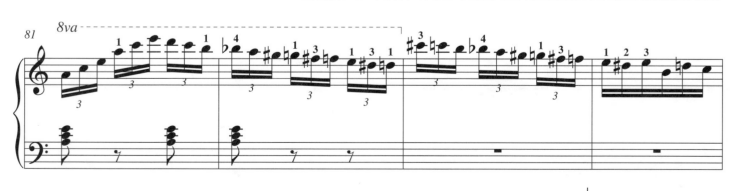

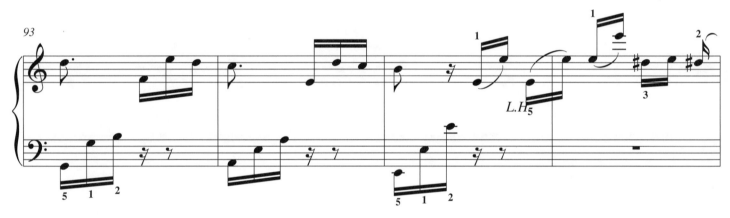